A WESTON MISCELLANY
by
The Weston Village Townswomen's Guild

First published by
Weston Village Townswomen's Guild in December 1999

Copyright © Weston Village Townswomen's Guild 1999

Weston Village Townswomen's Guild has asserted its right
under the Copyright, Designs and Patents Act, 1988,
to be identified as the Author of this work.

ISBN 1-899142-21-5

British Library Cataloguing in Publication Data
A catalogue record for this book is available from the
British Library

Copy-editing, book design and typesetting by
Mushroom Publishing
156 Southlands
Bath BA1 4EB
mail@mushroompublishing.com
http://www.mushroompublishing.com

Printed and bound by Redwood Books, Trowbridge

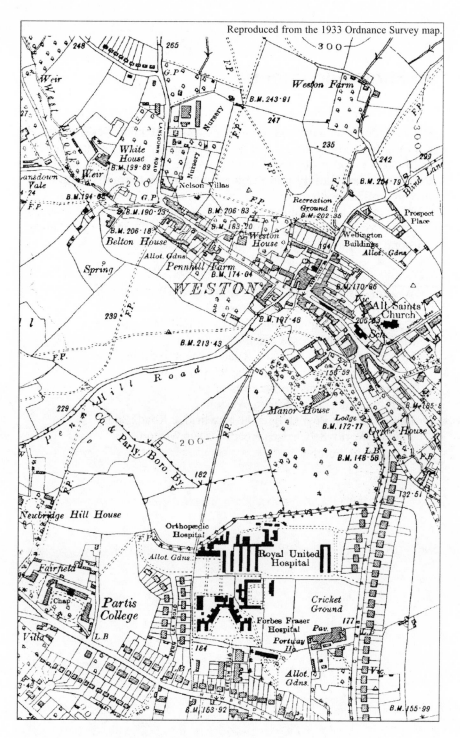

Ordnance Survey map of Weston (1933)

Acknowledgements

Weston Village Townswomen's Guild wishes to thank the many local residents who have given of their time and memories during the compilation of this book – if it had not been for their generosity this publication would not have been possible. We also wish to thank those who have kindly permitted the use of photographs from their private collections.

The Guild also wishes to extend its gratitude to all the local shops (listed below) who have generously agreed to sell copies of this book without any financial gain to themselves.

Weston Village Post Office, High Street, Weston
Jonquil, 1 Trafalgar Road, Weston
New Edition Hair Studios, 11 Crown Hill, Weston
St James Square Post Office
No.12 Hair Salon, Chelsea Road, Lower Weston
High Street Hardware, Brookside House, Weston
Ednas, 4 Brookside House, Weston
Bath Insurance, High Street, Weston
Lower Weston Post Office, 41 Newbridge Road, Bath
Flower World, 8e Chelsea Road, Lower Weston
Moravian Church

Contents

Introduction

This brief history of Weston, an ancient Somerset village near Bath, and the people who live there, has been compiled by members of the Weston Village Townswomen's Guild. The Townswomen's Guild is a national organisation that grew out of the aims of a group of women dedicated to creating higher opportunities for women, particularly in education. The first four Guilds were formed in 1928 after the full franchise was given to women in England, and a mandate was given by Parliament for funds to be used for the formation of experimental TGs. Today there are Guilds throughout the United Kingdom, their aims and interests covering practically every subject of interest to women and their families in a developing world.

The Weston Village Guild formed in 1950 as an afternoon guild, meeting monthly in All Saints Parish Hall. As membership of the new guild increased, many working women showed an interest, and it was decided to hold meetings in the evenings, originally in the Parish Hall. As membership increased, the WVTG moved to larger premises at the Moravian Church.

In 1980, at the request of local women who preferred to meet in the mornings, the Trafalgar Guild formed. They meet in the Parish Hall, and many of their memories are included here.

Today, Weston TG members come from a wide variety of backgrounds and occupations, and range in age from young housewives to octogenarians, whose long memories are well worth recording. Many hold down responsible jobs, but still find time to enjoy taking part in the activities of the Guilds. All help each other in times of need and are a very friendly and worthwhile company of women.

Although today many of the villagers are "incomers", there is still a strong village feeling among the people who live in and around Weston, and Guild members are very much a part of that. On Sundays, members attend All Saints or the Moravian Church, or the small Countess of Huntington's chapel in Trafalgar Road; they shop at local shops in the High Street, raise money for local charities and strongly support any petitions to the Council that affect their village.

Weston Village was named in the first Domesday Book survey in 1068, although it is known there was a settlement here before that. Over the years historians and local inhabitants, a number of whom have generously given permission for their memories to be published here, have recorded its past. But mainly these are the memories and experiences of past and present members of Weston Village Guilds during the later years of the twentieth century.

A Poem

A spinster, a wife, and a widow,
All lived in a street in our town,
The spinster was shy, the wife was young,
And the widow was lonely and down.

Now none of these three knew the others,
And their days were imperfectly filled,
Till someone had a great idea,
and started a Townswomen's Guild.

The spinster, the wife, and the widow
All went to the meeting and soon,
What a different life they were leading,
To each one the guild proved a boon.

The first went to classes in drama,
And even took part in a play,
The second got help with her cooking,
For ideas galore came her way.

The third found good friends all around her,
To help her along in her pain,
And all three were busy and useful
And life was worth living again.

There's so much we women can tackle,
So much to learn and to give
Whether spinster, or housewife, or widow,
The TG can help you to live.

A Stroll Through Weston

Starting at the Memorial end of the village, walk from the Royal United Hospital in Combe Park along the raised pavement. This has always had rails along it but it used to lead to a very different village. Stop at the bus stop, and look left: there was no busy main road there then, just a path leading up to Chubb's Farm where Greenbank Gardens is now. I can remember cows being led from the fields in Lucklands down through the village and up to the farm for milking! The Garage was still there with the old petrol pumps and of course, you were served! My husband can remember calling in for "a couple of shots" for his Vespa.

Where the bus stop is now there was a wooden door in what was then a very old stone wall. This led you up and through a lovely wood and eventually to the hospital. In the spring, this wood was full of snowdrops and crocuses – such a pretty sight. It was said that when a little child died in the hospital a nurse was sent down to the wood to pick a bunch of snowdrops to put in their hands.

Cross over the road to the Dentist. This was a grocer's shop run by a family called Williams, but I can never remember going in – not such the house on the opposite corner, which was the Manor Sweet Shop where I spent many happy times! The hairdressers next door was a bakery run by Mrs Hiskins. I can still see her with her crisp white coat, and the smell of newly baked bread was lovely! Notice the carved heads on the window frames; they have been there a long long time! In place of the Pet Shop and Chamberlain Videos there were houses.

Opposite the Memorial, coming down from Weston Park, was a Gentleman's Toilet, and this was closed not so long ago.

The newsagents was very much smaller, in fact there only seemed to be room for the lady, Mrs Perry, and her big book, in which she recorded all the newspaper accounts! The Post Office next door was a grocery shop owned by the Tucker family, and the actual Post Office was very tiny, entered from the pavement where the large window is now. You can imagine how crowded it became at Christmas when everyone was queuing to buy stamps, the queue used to be out onto the pavement! What a difference these days when you can buy stamps at many different shops.

The opening of the Somerfield Supermarket, Keymarkets as it was then, was a very exciting time. My children can remember people dressed as bears and tigers running around the village streets. We lined the playgroup children up to look over the wall and see the spectacular opening ceremony, which included the lion cubs from Longleat. Next door to

Keymarkets was a shoe shop, but it didn't stay in business very long. This was replaced by a hardware shop, owned by Mr and Mrs Poulson, who before this had a shop at the bottom of Trafalgar Road that was very small and crammed with all sorts of hardware from screws to galvanised buckets. They sold paraffin and I still think of that shop when I smell paraffin. Shops these days don't have that lovely old fashioned smell of the goods they sell, apart from I suppose Sainsburys, which I think deliberately wafts a smell of baked bread through the store to make you feel hungry.

The Co-op butchers was where the Insurance Brokers is now. When you went into that very small shop, you often came out covered in sawdust because as you queued you had to watch that you didn't brush against the carcases hung on the wall behind you. I wonder what the 'Public Health' would think now. The Co-op grocery store was where the entrance to Gainsborough Gardens is now. A charming man, Mr Leonard, who used to be the organist in St John's Church, Lower Weston, managed the shop.

Cross over and walk up Trafalgar Road. I love the handrail at the bottom of this street because it has been there for as long as I can remember, and looking up that street reminds me of what 'Old Weston' must have looked like.

John Brain had a greengrocer's shop at the top of Trafalgar Road, which is now replaced by flats. Next door to Mr Brain's shop was a house in which a lady lived who supposedly never came out, and the rumour goes that she was just like Miss Haversham of *Great Expectations* fame, who was jilted on her wedding day and there she stayed surrounded by her wedding day presents. This lady lived with her brother who kept pigs in an orchard at the back of the house, where Edgecombe Court is now. They also had a lovely bell, which hung on the wall in the lane at the side of the house, and the fun we had throwing stones at the bell to make it ring and then running away before he could catch us! Walk back down the road and you'll see on the right hand side the Countess of Huntingdon's Church, which is another reminder of 'Old Weston'.

Jonquil the florists was at one time a public house called The Queen's Head, and the paintwork advertising the pub name and Wills Cigarettes can still be seen faintly on the side wall. Later Mr Young the butcher took over the shop. It has always been very cold in there, which is good for the type of business that is there now. On the opposite corner to Jonquil, next to where Mr Poulson's original shop used to be, Lloyds Bank had a local branch, which was the only bank in the village apart from the Post Office and was very much missed when it closed.

The Parish Hall seems to have been there forever, and in fact it is only recently that new toilets have been added – before that it was a hazardous journey up some very dark crooked stairs. The stage remains the same, very small, but when you watch plays being performed on it by our talented Guild members, they cleverly hide the fact that it is so small. How they change costumes in the cold little room at the back is amazing. Also, the Guild holds very profitable coffee mornings in the hall twice a year. At Easter all the little tables are decorated with daffodils, the stalls sell lovely cakes and hot cross buns are served with coffee. At Christmas the whole hall is alive with tinsel and holly and even the stallholders themselves are decorated in a festive way, and everyone enjoys mince pies and coffee.

Mortimer's Yard was behind Jonquil, and the entrance and main yard was where Sheppards Gardens is now. All Mr Mortimer's equipment was coloured a very distinctive orange with black lettering.

Believe it or not but the little house next to the Dairy and opposite Brookside house was a Fish and Chip shop run by Mr Dyer and his wife. The fish and chips were really wrapped in newspaper, which somehow made them taste all the better!

Before the Brookside Shops were built, the Locks Brook ran along this part of the village. Lots of fun was had in the brook and in the field that led up from it to Southlands. But build the shops they did, and several changes have been seen since, from a 'Hygienic Laundry' where the baker's shop is now, and a greengrocers which is now the Tropical Fish Shop, but there has always been a Handyman Shop, Newsagents and Butchers. The shop that has never changed and is still named after the lady that first opened it is Ednas wool shop. Edna Luxton was a very valued Guild member and everyone that knew her remembers her with affection. Her very great experience in the art of flower arranging was eagerly sought by everyone, especially when Guild members entered the Bath Flower Show when as well as competing herself she was always willing to come into our tent and give us advice.

The house between Brookside and the Mazda Garage has always been known as Weston Farm House and I can remember at one time you could buy ice cream there, the sort that was wrapped in paper with two wafers to place either side.

From the Farm House I wander up the High Street and remember the smallest pub in Weston. It was called The Globe and is now a private residence, 82 High Street. It was so tiny you more or less had to sit outside, but I am told ladies could be taken through to the kitchen and be served lemonade! Opposite The Globe was a little greengrocers owned by a lady, Mrs Greenman. This was later a hairdressers before reverting back to a private house.

Here we are at the end of the village, now a roundabout, but in the old days the bus turned around here, and it was always referred to as "The End".

Memories of War

April 25th, 26th and 27th, 1942 will always be remembered in Bath as the time when the German planes dropped incendiary and high explosive bombs on the city, with tragic results. Weston, on the edge of the city, escaped fairly lightly, but the people never knew when to expect more raids, particularly from bombs jettisoned by the German planes returning to their bases.

Many families lost loved ones in the war. The granite War Memorial at the top of the High Street bears names from the First and Second World Wars, as well as the Korean War, paying tribute to those who gave their lives. However, the sacrifices of the village people should also be remembered and recorded for future generations.

Many of todays Townswomen have childhood memories of so many unexpected events which interrupted their schooldays, while others just old enough to join the services or take up nursing tell of the traumas of war in their own backyards, of adventures never hitherto imagined but not now forgotten, of friendships and romances which changed their lives.

Village children made new friends with children evacuated from big cities. Convalescent American soldiers sent to the American War Hospital in Combe Park were very popular with the children when they drove in jeeps through the village handing out chewing gum and sweets, which were severely rationed. For the mothers and housewives times were very hard because of rationing, queuing up every day for essential supplies. But they remained cheerful and prayed for it all to end.

Here, some members of Trafalgar Guild share their memories:

"The early forties found me evacuated with my firm and there I met my husband who joined the Home Guard and was assigned to an ack-ack battery. I thought it was a good idea to join the women's section of the Home Guard and was put in the signals section. This involved learning the Morse Code and then sending and receiving messages at 25 words per minute – on buzzer, lamp or flag. When we were sufficiently expert we had to take a Classification exam, which I remember vividly as it fell on my birthday, and I passed out in all three.

"We exercised with rather clumsy wireless sets and as D-Day approached we were instructed to send out masses of false messages with the idea that if any Germans picked up some of these they would

11

think them important, but actually we were jamming any vital information – though I don't think we were aware of this at the time. We were also taught how to hold and fire a .22 rifle, which was incredibly heavy and had a nasty kickback. We were only allowed old used cards for target practice and when mine was returned to me I saw I had managed to get inside the circle, but someone had scored a bull's eye before me and that someone was Warwick Deacon who was nicknamed 'Deadshot Deacon'. I became Mrs Deacon in 1947."

Another member will never forget coming home for lunch one day with her father: "We were served with a delicious looking meal of fried steak, fried onions, mashed potatoes and vegetables. As the meat ration at the time was really meagre, we were very surprised and my mother told us the meat was an extra perk from the butcher, and Dad and I tucked in with relish. During the afternoon I suffered an occasional burp, but blamed the onion. Later, Mother confessed our delicious steak had been whale meat, which she couldn't bring herself to eat, knowing what it was. When the butcher gave her some more, none of us could eat it, and I said it had tasted like cod-liver oil."

Another member was married in November 1940, and moved into her new home in Newbridge Road. Just six weeks later a planeload of stray bombs was dropped as the Germans returned home and one landed at the back of her garden. Luckily, it did not explode, but having an unexploded bomb in the garden meant leaving the house and staying with her mother-in-law. Soon afterwards, her husband left for Normandy with the Army, and came through the war safely to return home.

As well as jobs in the Civil Service, nursing, and the Forces, women took on a great variety of jobs to free men for the Forces and sometimes even to free other women for special jobs. One such lady worked on the railways for GWR after her father refused to sign the form for her to join the services. Instead, the stationmaster offered her a job selling tickets and she worked twelve-hour shifts. Once a month she had to open up Oldfield Park Halt single-handed, which meant starting work at 5.30am. In this job, she had to do everything from issuing tickets to closing the train doors and she enjoyed it all tremendously.

A Brief History of Weston Schools

Before schools, the local parson or vicar would have given what education was available, and as most people had little or no interest in learning, no school had been necessary.

Education in the mid Eighteenth century was usually given in "Dames" schools – establishments run in the main by frail spinster women who could not manage heavier work. Children were taught in these women's own homes. There are no records of any payments to these teachers.

Weston village did not boast a school until 1745, when mention of a "Choole" was made in the Parish records. The record states that a broken window cost 1/- for a "skein of Helme" (thatch), and 7½ feet of glass at 6d a foot plus labour charges to mend it.

In 1795 Miss Resbury Hocker started a school in The Grove. She was helped by Baron Daly who established free schools in various cottages around Weston and encouraged the education of children up to the age of 12 years. Teachers were paid the princely sum of 3/- a quarter. Miss Hocker died in 1802 – she had been a great benefactor, and left many books to the community.

Between 1802 and 1814 there was no school at all in the village, but it was reported late in 1814 that "the laudable design of establishing a charity school on Dr Bell's system in the populous Parish of Weston met with good support" and that "a Schoolroom would shortly be erected, capable of containing 120 children". Therefore, the National Society was approached and, in 1817, the Parish Hall was built and used as the village school.

In 1830, a Mr Browning established a commercial school at The Batch. This was a boarding school and pupils were housed in The Grove and Trafalgar Road. The Headmaster, Mr George, lived in Lansdown House. Mr Albert succeeded Mr George but he resigned in 1891 and built the Homestead. When Mr Cloutte became headmaster of the school it did not prosper and he resigned in 1897. It finally closed down in 1903.

A contemporary of the Browning school was the Portway Middle Class Boarding School, which was housed in Combe Park. It opened in 1868 and the fees were five guineas a quarter for children under nine years old. We are told that the pupils attended All Saints Church and were regularly chastised for sitting in the gallery and firing pellets at the parish clerk. Sometime in the late 1800s it was taken over by Mrs

Cloutte who established a girls' school there. Finally, in 1898, it was purchased by Chivers the bookbinders.

Mr William Daw became headmaster of Weston Village School in 1878. He was a strict disciplinarian and remained at the school until 1919, when Mr Bryant succeeded him. The village school remained in the buildings we now know as the Parish Hall and the Church Centre until 1957 when it moved to Broadmoor Lane.

During talks with several villagers who attended the schools at various times between 1918 and 1960, the following stories have been remembered. In 1918, on entering the School (now the Church Centre), the middle portion was the head teacher's living quarters. Other teachers were housed next door to the Post Office. To the left was the girls' school and to the right the infants department. The boys were kept well away on the other side. The boys' headmaster at this time was Mr Daw. He was not remembered too kindly by our informants, who recalled a parent confronting the Headmaster with his son and displaying the dreadful weals across his back – the result of an over zealous caning by Mr Daw.

Miss Turner was the girls' headmistress and was not very popular. Miss Yaxley was the infants' headmistress and Miss Frayling, Miss Browning and Miss Henstey, who taught cookery, also helped with the infants. Our informants had prayers every morning, and because it was a Church School, they attended the Church for all major religious occasions. Besides religion, the other subjects taught were basic arithmetic, writing, history, geography, singing, sewing and housewifery. Children sat on a three-legged stool and wrote with chalk on a slate. It was remembered as being very cold with only a boiler to warm the room. Chilblains were very commonplace among the pupils.

Cookery and housewifery were taught in the Parish Hall. A former pupil remembers well how pleased all her class were when a particularly disliked teacher tasted a friend's cake only to find that the girl had added salt to the mixture instead of sugar! Poetry was most important in the lives of the students and long recitations were learnt parrot fashion in the same way that times tables were chanted.

One teacher would take all subjects including physical education, which was performed in the playground. School Sports Day took place on the Thursday before Whit Sunday at the Recreation Ground. On Empire Day all pupils had to walk around the Union Flag and salute.

Many pupils spoke of the very long journeys made by some pupils – always on foot. They came to Weston from places like Langridge, Kelston, Newton-St-Loe and other outlying villages. As there were no school dinners pupils were allowed to bring packed lunches – usually bread and dripping or bread and cheese. One young boy, a cripple, made the daily journey to school from Kelston on crutches.

Miss Yaxley's class at All Saints School in 1930 (from the collection of Victor Rose).

Few pupils really enjoyed school and their memories are of being cold, learning tables, doing lines and having the cane. Several ex-pupils felt that because Weston All Saints was a Church school, religion was forced down their throats.

Apparently, school prizes were only given to the head boy or head girl, but lesser students were able to get Sunday School prizes for regular attendance or good behaviour. Books were not allowed to be taken home but reading was encouraged; sometimes the pupils were given a book to read whilst the teacher was absent from the class, but not much learning was done because the children were too busy throwing chalk or other projectiles at each other!

There was no sex education, and as one lady pointed out to us "you just had to learn about it the nasty way". It was a dreadful thing if a girl got herself into trouble – true to form the boy had nothing to do with the conception. It was also a terrible stigma if you received a letter from the 'nit nurse' – you were considered dirty and immediately ostracized. Both the dentist (or 'the butcher' as he was affectionately known) and the nit nurse provided a free service.

It seems that Weston School had a very bad reputation, and some parents sent their children by free bus to Widcombe School instead.

During the 1920s, pupils could obtain clothing cards, about the size of a postcard. Each week children could take money to school and have their card stamped. At the end of the year the card was totalled and families purchased clothes from certain shops in Bath – a lifeline for large families.

By the 1930s there was mixed education right through school, and pre-school started at 3 years of age. The morning session was from 9am to 12pm. The afternoon session began with an hour's sleep on camp beds or blankets on the floor.

It was during this period that Polly Parsons was teaching at the school. She was very keen on her pupils learning tables. Other teachers remembered at this time were Crabby Davis, Dinky Dando who caned naughty children, Miss Brown and Don Sparkes, who taught woodwork. All these taught in the junior school.

By 1952 the Infants school was housed in what is now the Scout Hall. In 1957 the school moved to its present site in Broadmoor Lane. At this time Weston All Saints was still not considered a good school academically and many parents elected to send their children to Newbridge School. Mr Pike was the headmaster of the mixed junior school.

Other teachers remembered during this period were Mr Jones who was Welsh and always made the pupils sing Welsh songs, Mrs Pendlebury whose motto was "Good, Better, Best, Never let it rest, 'til your Good is Better and your Better Best!" Miss Osbourne drilled the children on how to behave when the school inspectors visited – they would rehearse the answers to questions. Other memories included drinking luke warm milk that had been stored too near the boiler.

In 1971, the school divided into the Weston County Infants under the Headship of Miss Jean Flood and the Weston All Saints Junior School under the Headship of Mr Andrew. In approximately 1985 the two schools were reunited as Weston All Saints Primary School. To bring Weston All Saints Primary School's history completely up to date, it is encouraging to note that in recent years, under the Headship of Mrs Bull, the school has cast off its former reputation, and is now one of the most respected schools in the city having won, in 1992, the National Schools Curriculum Award.

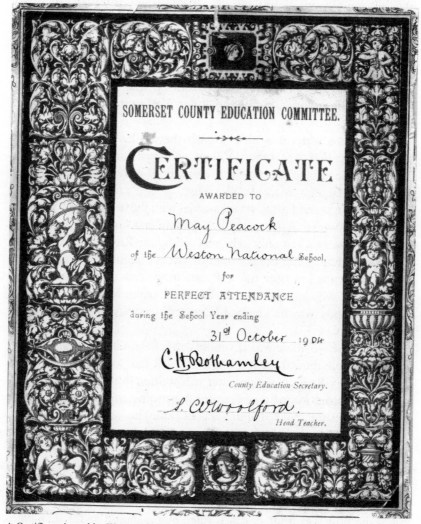

A Certificate issued by Weston National School in 1904 (from the collection of Victor Rose)

The Weston Brook

Walk along Broadmoor Lane to the end and then turn right up a small country lane. Halfway up, still gushing out of the bank, is the source of the village brook, water so sparkling and clear you are still tempted to drink it, as I did as a child. It was also very useful for washing bicycles, after riding through the muddy lanes.

It is difficult to imagine now, but in the sixteenth century this brook ran along Broadmoor Lane, through the farmland, which now belongs to John Osborne, along through the village to the Mill that was where Montrose Cottages now stand. From there, it wound its way through Gainsborough Gardens and eventually down to Lower Weston. The Brook was then called "Lox Brook".

Several streams also ran into this brook, one down the line of the present Trafalgar Road, and another from Lucklands. It was probably very dry in the summer, but in the winter Weston must have been very wet indeed.

With all this water it is little wonder that in the nineteenth century Weston was called the Laundry Village, with washing often hung out to dry across the village streets. But the supply of water to the houses was most unsatisfactory, as was the drainage.

There were several disasters connected with the brook. In 1828 a man fell in and drowned. After a very heavy thunderstorm in 1878 a boy fell in and was swept away only to be rescued by the Rev. Edward Wilkins, who was watching the flood from his garden. Seeing the child's great danger he jumped in from the wall, and at the risk of his own life rescued the boy, who later became the father of Arthur Mortimer. After this episode the boy was nicknamed "Ducker" (see also 'The Pageant of Weston' on page 37).

Earlier, in 1846, there was an outbreak of cholera in the West Country. Twenty people died from it in the Bristol Road, and there were four deaths in the village. A strong letter was written to the Vestry, suggesting the construction of a sewer and the piping of pure water to the village. The estimated cost of this was £1,000. The Vestry suggested that a very modified scheme of cleansing the brook be carried out, but that bringing a better supply of water to the village must be left until such time as the state of Law or finances at their disposal would enable them to carry out the elaborate and expensive operation.

However, in 1872, the water was piped down and through the village, but as the flow was limited, it was ruled that it should be for standpipes and street pumps only. One of these pumps can still be seen at the bottom of Trafalgar Road.

The brook ran through the village, gushing from a waterfall by the White House at the end (unfortunately both are now gone). Then the brook carried on its course to where the Brookside Shops now stand.

What fun we had there building dams to try and flood the village – fortunately without success! This childhood revelry was stopped for us in 1954 when the brook was diverted under the road into pipes.

However, that didn't stop the floods. In July 1968, an abnormal rain-storm badly flooded the village, particularly Montrose Cottages. I can still smell those carpets all laid on the walls to dry in the sun that shone the next day. Different to the sixteenth century, when probably rolls of cloth were laid to dry.

Wessex Water did major works in the village in 1991, and after very heavy rainstorms in December 1992, when there were floods elsewhere, Weston was Free and Dry!

Weston High Street from the War Memorial, probably 1968 (from the collection of Victor Rose)

A Nurse at War: 1938-1944

In late 1938 my friend Win and I heard about a group called the CNR, which turned out to be the Civil Nursing Reserve. Having always thought we would like nursing, we decided to join up. It involved lectures, practical classes, theory lessons etc, for six or seven months, and by now we were well into 1939. We then had two exams to do, and towards the end, we had to do 96 hours in a hospital of their choice, which was roughly two weeks without pay. I had to save like mad for a couple of months to be able to pay my mother, but it was worth it in the end. I was sent to the Orthopaedic Hospital. While there, we had to do a spell on the children's ward, the adult ward, and the longer-term patients, and watch an operation, which I nearly fell down on. The colour didn't come back into my cheeks for 3 days, but I liked it. Then, with your exam results, and the Matron's report on you, you either passed or not. Everyone knew by now what the outcome was going to be, and war was finally declared on September 3rd. So we were called up, issued with our uniforms, indoor and out, and pages of instructions, then thrown in at the deep end.

We had both put in to be mobile, thinking it would be more interesting. So I was sent to the town of Street, and Win went to St. Martin's Hospital. I went to The Grange, a big, rambling old place, commandeered as an emergency hospital – quite a few sprang up around the country. I can't say I enjoyed it, as going into 1940 was a very cold winter, and no central heating. I went to bed with clothes on, and my dressing gown, plus a hot water bottle, and was still cold. I had one half day a week, and one day off a month, which once a month I joined together and came home. Stan used to come to Wells on Saturday afternoon, and I would bus from Street, then we both got on another bus back to Bath. At that time we mostly had evacuees, and accidents from the factory. While there, I also became a blood donor.

Then my father died at the beginning of 1940, and my eldest brother was called up in March, leaving my mother with a very young brother and sister. This in turn gave me the opportunity to apply for a transfer back to Bath on compassionate grounds. The 'powers that be' finally granted it, and two or three months later I was back in Bath and heading for St. Martin's Hospital. By this time they had built the new wing, which very soon was filled with Dunkirk veterans. They were called the 'Boys in Blue' because as soon as they were able to get up, they were given white shirts and blue suits to wear. The majority were a long way from home, but they were a good crowd, and we all helped them out, as they did us. They would take the tea trolleys around, and fetch and carry for their mates, while we took them for walks or into the town, and invited them to our homes for tea, and they appreciated it. Rationing had started, and we were all getting used to dried egg, whale meat, and the inevitable Spam!

By now I was doing night duty, and what a difference! First of all we had the blackout to contend with, and the stoves in the ward. They were huge black monsters; one near the top of the ward and one near the bottom. Of course, there was no central heating, so we had to keep them going all night. The porters brought buckets of coke before going off duty, and we used to wrap a blanket round our legs, and sit in the dark. It was a twelve-hour shift, 8pm to 8am, and most nights we were very busy, but we had two nights a week off. We began to take in civilian casualties, and a few little incidents took place – they were mostly on night duty. But 1940 drew to a close, and soon we were into 1941, and I was back on day duty again. A Dr Kohn – he was a Czech refugee – joined the staff. A brilliant doctor, everyone liked him. Not so his understudy, a young, tall, dark and handsome man, who seemed to rub everyone up the wrong way, including me! In the meantime, Eileen, the girl next door, and I, had joined the ARP, and our post was only about five minutes away. There was a good crowd of Helpers, Nurses, First Aid men, etc, and we all had to do a night's duty once a week, and also attend a class on gas precautions. So, with this and our hospital work, we were kept quite busy. There were four of us on our ward, Nurses Jenner, Churchill, and Russ – or Rusty as she was affectionately called. We got on well together and weathered several incidents. Then on 7th December, the Japanese bombed Pearl Harbor, bringing America into the war, and so the year passed into 1942.

Well, as you all know, the Luftwaffe paid us a visit on Saturday, April 25th. First we heard the sirens, which we were used to, but this time the bombs were meant for us. I went to get my little brother up, then Eileen and I ran to the ARP post, only to discover that a bomb had dropped at the end of the Paragon. It was a direct hit, right opposite our road. A Dr Mary Middlemas, her two sisters and two maids, were all killed, but in the house next door, in the basement, which was partly demolished, was a family of four. The parents were both dead, and one little girl, so we took the other one to the casualty station, but sad to say, she eventually died as well. Then, just before daybreak, the bombers went away and we all went home. Me, to find that our front windows were blown in, as were Eileen's, and my pillows and bed were covered with shards of glass. We all had to find our way to work next day, as there were no buses. The Bear Flat was a mass of flames, rubble, fire engines with hoses snaking everywhere, and bleary-eyed men, but as we had our uniforms on, they let us through. And when we had done our days duty, and looked forward to a nice sleep, back came the bombers, just after midnight. It was a shorter raid, but much more deadly. The bombs just rained down, casualties were heavy, and damage severe. But they finally went away, and things gradually returned to normal. A week or so later, the King and Queen paid us a visit, and I was back on night duty.

We were always very busy at the hospital; as soon as we sent a dozen boys home another dozen came in. Some would never fight again, but they were mostly very appreciative, obliging, and well behaved. On the lighter side, two or three romances came to fruition, and in June Hitler sounded his own death knell by invading Russia. There were always little incidents happening, but we all began to think of eventual victory, and the George Cross was awarded to the island of Malta. Then once again it was Christmas, and into another new year – 1943.

The big event for me was my own wedding in January. There was snow on the ground and it was very cold. Nurses Churchill and Rusty came, and although everything was in short supply, all relatives and friends chipped in, and a good time was had by all. I even had quite a nice wedding cake, as my brother-in-law was a master baker. I was allowed one day off for the wedding, and one day for the honeymoon, so we went, of all places, to London for the day. Then it was back to work, and even more work, as trainloads of men were coming in every week. The Battle of the Atlantic was going full blast, and Monty was winning in North Africa. In June, Italy was invaded by the Allies, and they surrendered in September. In fact, all the news was very encouraging, and I was back on night duty again. We were being rushed off our feet, but still enjoying it.

And so the year rattled away into 1944 and for the first time, I must say, there were signs of weariness in everyone. There was sickness among the staff, there were a number of strikes. Even the children didn't escape as the school leaving age was raised to 15. But for me, I found I was three months pregnant, and quite happy about it, although you supposed it was expected of you to work as long as possible. So at the end of March I gave in my notice, and at the end of April, I left St Martin's Hospital with a tinge of regret. I was given a lovely folding camera by the boys, which I still have, but can't use. And on 9th June my son John was born in Stratton House, which is now a retirement home. One last little item of news, at our VE Day party the next year, my son won third prize in a baby competition.

A Stroll Around the Churchyard

All Saints Church, the parish church of Weston, stands high on a hill overlooking the village. It has a very attractive approach, in fact a perfect setting for a wedding or, as happened once, a TV film set!

During her lifetime Jane Austen visited the churchyard and I am sure little has changed since then. The churchyard was closed for burials in 1876, when it had been used as a burial place for over 600 years. It has been estimated that some ten thousand internments were made during that time.

This peaceful place amongst the yew trees still has many interesting gravestones. Some show how many children died so young. One stone belonging to the Adams family tells us that all their three children died before they were four years old.

In one corner lie the Military graves. One very ornate one, with fine carvings of a musket, rifle, cannon, sword etc, belongs to "General Joseph Smith, a brave officer who died in 1790".

Another imposing monument is that of Philip Affleck, Admiral of the White Squadron, who died in 1799, aged 74 years.

The grave that is said to be the oldest in the churchyard and looks, I think, like an Egyptian Mummy, lies under a yew tree at the top of the churchyard by the Kissing Gate. Do take a look at this gate – it is really lovely.

Dr William Oliver, physician, had property in Weston. He helped found Bath Hospital, but is perhaps better known as the inventor of the famous Bath Oliver biscuit. He died in 1870 and his grave lies by the vestry door. There is another memorial to him inside the church almost opposite to this grave outside, but it is very high up on the wall and difficult to read.

The Mistress of Weston Infant School had a stone laid in her memory by the Vicar of the Parish: Elizabeth Hyett, who died in 1873, was Mistress of the School for 21 years.

Some of the graves have very long and meaningful epitaphs like this one:

A Soul Prepared, need no delay
The Summons came, the Saints Obey
Quick was the passage, narrow was the road
He shuts his eyes and wakes with God!

These are just a few of the notable graves, but do take a longer look, the carvings and epitaphs are so interesting.

Let us go inside the Church. Once inside, turn right and look up at the first stained glass window called 'The St Alphege Window'. This commemorates the famous saint who, according to tradition, was born in Weston.

The second window reads

> "In Memory of Sidney Nutcombe of Templecombe House,
> Templecombe: Accidentally killed April 27th 1898, Aged
> 28. In the midst of life, we are in Death."

A tablet near the 'little' door of the church reads that it was placed to record a legacy of £300 left by the Rt Hon Lady Mary Stanley in trust to the Ministers/Churchwardens of the Parish, who are directed out of the interest arising from it, to keep her Ladyship's tomb in the church-yard in repair and to give the residue to the poor! I cannot find the tombstone, but I am told the fund to the poor was only ended a few years ago.

Opposite this tablet is a fine monument to Alderman Sherston, Mayor of Bath, who died in 1641.

Some more elaborate epitaphs include:

> "Sacred to the memory of Thomas Peterson Esq of this
> parish. Died April 19th 1803, age 42.
> When death from God above,
> So Suddenly to Part our Love,
> No Friends nor yet Physicians art
> Could prevent the fatal dart."

> "Eleanor Matilda Maria – fifth daughter of Charles and
> Emma Parry, born June 8th 1822, died April 28th 1840.
> Calm on the Bosom of thy God
> Fair Spirit Rest thee now
> E'en while with ours thy footsteps trod
> His seal was on thy brow
> Dust to its Narrow House Beneath
> Soul to its Place on High
> They that have seen thy Look in Death
> No more may fear to die."

Up in the Gallery can be found this memorial to Christina Guliana Gaskell, who died March 24th 1803, aged 69.

"Only daughter of William Penn Esq. of Shanagarry in the County of the Cork, the Grandson of William Penn, the founder and first proprietor of the City of Philadelphia, a Province of Pennsylvania in America."

Above the main door is a memorial to:

"George Middleton, Banker in London, nearly related to the Earl of Middleton but truly enrobed by divine Charity grafted upon happy nature. His sorrowful widow erected for him this plain Monument, suitable to that humbly, Simplicity of Manners which were so conficious of his character. 1740." (Notice the Gentleman's Hat, typical of those worn at that time).

These are only a few of the many interesting epitaphs inside the Church. Do have a look for some more, and try and find this one:

"Near this place, are deposited the remains of Lt Col Fleming Martin, many years Chief Engineer on the Bengal Establishment in the service of the Hon East Indies Company, he died 18 July 1799. Aged   years."
(Was his age unknown?)

Geography Of Weston

Weston is about 2½ miles from the centre of Bath in a north-west direction, and should not be confused with Weston-super-Mare, the resort on the Bristol Channel.

Weston covers quite a large area, being bounded roughly by Walcot (there is still a stone boundary marker in Weston Road near Moravian Cottages), the Bristol Avon, Kelston and Lansdown (there are Turnpike Trust posts on the road to Kelston and also near Beckford's Tower, Lansdown).

In the 1800s, as Bath grew westwards, St John's Parish Church was built, thus creating a separate parish of Lower Weston in 1878 on land previously within Weston parish. It should be noted that there is no separate parish of Upper Weston.

However, Weston village, whilst now a part of Bath and also having lost a lot of its older buildings through redevelopment, can still be identified quite clearly thanks largely to being in a valley and still being surrounded by green fields and hills.

The old village is mainly in an area bounded by All Saints Church, Montrose Cottages and the bottom of Lansdown Lane. To the west is Penn Hill and Dean Hill (approx 120 and 180 metres high), to the north and east are Lansdown (approx 230 metres) and Primrose Hill, whilst to the south most of the area is now developed with housing and the Royal United Hospital. In general, the village buildings followed the line of the street, now High Street, and even today some still run off at right angles from this street.

The High Street followed the line of Locks (Lox) Brook, which many older inhabitants still remember as being open, but today it is mostly piped underground. The brook was fed by the many springs, which still rise in the hills around the village. When the brook overflowed in times of flood, Church Street (The Batch) provided a relatively dry route due to its additional height.

Farming has always been important to Weston and even today there are farms, mainly cattle, very close by. The High Street still has some farm buildings from earlier years, for example, Penn Farmhouse and also buildings to the back of the dairy opposite Brookside House.

Weston is on the edge of the Cotswolds and is on the Cotswold Way, which descends from Penn Hill across the village and then up Sion Hill, en-route to Bath. The older buildings, which are easily recognizable, reflect the connection between Weston, Bath and the Cotswolds as some are built with oolite or Bath stone whilst others are built with local lias stone similar to the Cotswold villages. There is evidence of quarrying in Lansdown and to the south side of the Homestead, Combe Park.

Listed Buildings

Listed buildings are noted for their special architectural or historic interest and fall into four broad categories:

a. Buildings of significance pre-1700.
b. Good buildings, mostly intact, dated 1700-1840. These buildings may be quite modest.
c. Buildings of definite quality and character dated 1840-1914; also major works of important architects.
d. Key buildings 1914-1939.

Weston Village has about 70 Listed Buildings – all Grade II:

- Most of the houses are in the High Street. Others are in Trafalgar Road and near All Saints Church. These, in the main, are composed of attractive cottages and terraced houses.
- In addition to the houses, there are a few more prestigious listed dwellings: the Countess of Huntingdon's Chapel in Trafalgar Road, The Vicarage and Church Hall, All Saints Church, and the drinking fountain in the wall in front of the Church Centre in the High Street.
- The three village public houses are also listed – The King's Head and The Crown & Anchor in the High Street, and The Old Crown on Crown Hill are also listed.

At the beginning of this century, inhabitants of these listed houses included labourers, laundresses, masons, plasterers, carters, coal merchants and shopkeepers. Also seamstresses, gardeners, a locksmith and a watchman.

From 1910 onwards are mentioned brewers, farriers, smiths, a policeman, a postman, a cellarman – and by 1930 a dairyman and a Captain of Fire Brigade.

Memories of the Great Flood in 1968

Weeks of heavy rain had saturated the hills.

On this particular Wednesday, we journeyed to Longwell Green, a village about 10 miles away, to take my mother home. We started back to Weston about 9.30pm. All roads were flooded, it was raining heavily, and there was a great deal of thunder and forked lightening. Ours was the last car to be allowed down Willsbridge Hill, and we decided to return on the Keynsham Road rather than go through Bitton and Swineford. Several vehicles went together in single file, with policemen along the route shouting out to everyone to keep to the centre of the road. We managed to get back to Penn Lea Road, about half a mile from our house, where we were stopped by police and told to leave the car and walk the rest of the way into Weston. There were several others doing the same.

The village High Street was a rushing torrent of waist-high water. To cross, we linked arms with a policeman, who begged us to take small, slow steps, or our legs would go from under us. Thankfully we made it safely, and then had to climb two garden walls to reach Wellington Buildings, which is the next street to Brookfield Park where we live. We moved on to Brookfield Park to find another river, and beyond it our house with water pouring out of the front door. As soon as we got in, we hurriedly turned off the electricity at the mains, and went to find torches and candles. We heard children screaming next door and went to investigate, where we found that the torrent coming down the hill had burst open their back door, and the key had fallen in the water. Their father was away doing a night shift at work. We found their key, and the children quietened down and settled with their mother. We went back to our own house and found two elderly ladies standing in our porch, very wet and cold. As it was still raining, and it was impossible for them to get back into the village, they came into the house, through the six inches of water in the hallway. We offered them the spare room for the night, with a double bed, which they gratefully accepted.

They were up early the next morning, when, thank goodness, the water had gone down, and had some tea and toast. They thanked us and said goodbye, then to our surprise, one went one way and one went the other. We were very curious, but a letter and a box of chocolates a couple of days later explained everything. It turned out they had not known each other.

But for us, we had to begin the task of cleaning up – and what a job! Everything was plastered in mud, and the carpets completely soaked. It took six of us to lift the lounge carpet and carry it outside because of the added weight of water. But help was at hand! The TG played badminton in the village hall on Thursday mornings, and as soon as they heard of our trouble, they came to help. One went home, collected old towels from her neighbours, then turned-to and started to wash all the chairs and table legs. Another cooked us a tray of sausage rolls and fairy cakes. Several others helped as well. It was so heart-warming.

The crunch came about a month later, when the kitchen floor tiles started to buckle, so we had to have new tiles laid. Later still, we found that several floorboards had rotted from the damp. But things eventually got back to normal, though it must be said it was an experience we shall never forget.

This Tells An Intriguing Story!

December 1765. Expences for William Cox, and Self and Horse in going to Shipton Mallet and taking Jonathan Millard and bringing him to Weston	£1:10:0
for a gard and expences on Jonathan Millard at Shipton ...	£0:7:4
Expences on the road for Ditto	£0:1:0
for a Horse for him to ride	£0:3:6
for Hay and Corn to keep the Horse 1 night	£0:1:0
for a man to have the Horse home	£0:4:2
for eating drinking lodging and time	£0:3:1
for 2 men to gard Jonathan Millard the 1st night	£0:4:0
for 2 men to gard him next day	£0:2:4
for his examination and expences	£0:5:2
for 2 men to gard him 2nd night	£0:4:0
for the licence	£1:8:6
Paid Jonathan Millard to marry Mary Parris	£2:2:0
To the Parson	£0:5:0
To the Clark	£0:2:6
To Jonathan Millard to bear his expences home	£0:2:6
Expences of setting them off	£0:2:6
for a Horse to carry the woman home	£0:7:6
for a man to go home with her	£0:4:0
Expences for Man and Horse on the road	£0:4:0
Expences for Jonathan Millard and two men to gard him at the Blew Lodge being there one night and part of 2 days	£0:17:6
Paid to Thomas Cox for attending at the examination of Jonathan Millard and Mary Parris and at getting the licence for Self attending a Bord	£0:2:6

The Inclusion of Weston into Bath

On October 26, 1950, Royal Assent was given to the Bath Extension Act. On April 1, 1951, the boundary of the existing City of Bath would be altered. In addition to the existing City, parts of the Parishes of Charlecombe, Claverton, Englishcombe, Monkton Combe and Weston would be included. This was an additional area of 1,130 acres. The special Boundaries Committee of Bath City Council met on November 20, 1950 and decided that there was to be a meeting with the affected Parishes in the following January 1951.

There seems to have been a mixed reaction to the proposed boundary alterations, from both Bath and Weston. The concerns were mainly of a financial nature. Bath residents were concerned that Weston would be a financial liability for maybe ten to fifteen years, until standards in education, drainage, roads and lighting were brought up to Bath City level. Weston residents were concerned that their rates would rise.

To alleviate some of these worries, Councillor E H Cox of Bath City Council spoke to a large and lively audience in the Weston Assembly Hall on October 23, 1950. It was stated that Parish Councillors and rural Councillors would continue to represent their remaining areas until their normal period of retirement.

The Bath Evening Chronicle reported on April 2, 1951 that eight Parish Councillors from Weston, led by Mr W W Blake, Chairman, walked to Weston All Saints Church. They attended a takeover service together with the Mayor of Bath, Councillor Miss Kathleen Harper, plus members and officials of Bath City Council.

Apparently, Mr Blake was a staunch opponent of the takeover, and as a last Parish Council duty had asked all his councillors to attend the service.

The Vicar, Rev E J Rowe, did not refer to the takeover in his sermon. After the service, the Mayor shook hands with all the parishioners as they left and the church bells were rung.

Weston Free Church

Weston Free Church is so called because it was built at a time when there was a considerable expansion of housing in the community, to serve the needs of people of the Free Churches tradition (Methodist, Baptist, Congregational, etc., and of course Moravian). The Moravians received the support of the other members of the Free Church Council in Bath and so, whilst being organized as a congregation of the Moravian Church, the name Free Church was retained to indicate its broader base.

The Moravian Church is a pre-Reformation Church, founded in 1457 as part of the movement that grew from the teaching and influence of Jan Hus, the great Czech preacher who was rector of Prague University and a great admirer of his English contemporary Wycliffe. Hus was martyred in 1415 but his death lit a flame that was to burn fiercely in central Europe. Disorganized by persecution, the refugees came from Bohemia, Poland and Moravia and found a home on the estates of a pious Saxon nobleman, Count Nicholas von Zinzendorf, the 300th anniversary of whose birth will be commemorated in 2000. Zinzendorf formed them into a coherent body again in the early eighteenth century, which is also when the Moravian Church came to England. Here it was recognized by Act of Parliament, the Acta Fratrum of 1749, as an ancient, Protestant, Episcopal Church.

Moravian bishops do not have a diocese but are elected by the synod and assume their Episcopal duties in addition to whatever they are doing, pastoral or administrative. The Church's worship is more liturgical than the average Free Church, but at the same time, we enjoy a great deal of freedom in this respect. The Church is mainstream in its belief and is not doctrinaire in its approach. We welcome all fellow-Christians who wish to join us at the Lord's Table. The great sixteenth century educationalist and bishop, Jan Amos Comenius (Komensky) handed on a saying, which sums up our attitude: "In things essential, unity; in things non-essential, liberty; in all things charity."

The Moravians played a prominent part in the eighteenth century Evangelical Revival in England. Famously it was at a Moravian meeting in Aldersgate, London, that John Wesley "felt his heart strangely warmed". They had a powerful effect on the Wesley brothers and were thus, to borrow a phrase, the midwives of the Methodist movement. Other great evangelistic preachers at the time were George

Whitfield and John Cennick. Cennick preached widely in Wiltshire and Ireland. He founded a society in Bath in 1752, which became the first Moravian congregation in 1765. They met in Monmouth Street, and when this became too small built the church in Charlotte Street, now offices next door to the Registrar's. This served as the Moravian Church from 1834 to 1910. In 1907, the Coronation Avenue church was built and in 1953 the congregation in Weston was founded. Our church building was completed in 1956/7 to mark the quincentenary of the Moravian Church.

Most of the money to finance the Weston building came from War Damage compensation for the bombing of the Church headquarters at Fetter Lane in London (off Fleet Street). The Fetter Lane congregation, the oldest in the British Province, now meets in Chelsea. There is a brick encased in the wall inside the Weston church that came from the original Fetter Lane building.

We try to serve the community in Weston in various ways. One of the links that we value is with the local Townswomen's Guild. Boys' Brigade, Parent & Toddler Group, Shoppers' Creche, Lunch Fellowship, and so on, serve other needs. We try to show the meaning of Christian love and fellowship in the lives of members, and when we meet together. Whilst some differences are regrettable where they make for division and discord, we rejoice in the God-given diversity of humanity, and when reflected in the Church, recognize it as a cause for thanksgiving and a source of strength.

We wish our local Townswomen's Guild a Happy 50th Anniversary. May the happy association between us continue from strength to strength.

The Flower Show

In 1986 the Carnival Committee asked Vera Payne of Jonquils to run a flower show, and they would stand the cost. It was a great success and was again organised in 1987 under the same format.

The Carnival did not take place in 1988 and so the Flower Show Committee decided to carry on on their own. It has been running successfully ever since, and is enjoyed by many. A distribution of the profits are given to village groups every year.

Doug Symonds is the present chairman.

Norma's Weston

I came to live in Holcombe Green, Weston when I was eight years old. Having spent those first eight years living in a flat in Sydney Place, Bathwick, the first thing I did was to ride my little bike around Holcombe Green. Oh, the freedom I felt, out on my own and going home to a *house*, with my own bedroom and a garden to play in. The fun we had in that garden when my sister and I became friends with the neighbour's children. My fondest memories are of making miniature gardens to enter in the Weston Carnival Garden Show – everyone in Weston seemed to enter that show. My brother was entered for the Bonniest Baby! There were competitions for the best vegetables, vases of wild flowers, and handicrafts. Every time I enter a tent now I still smell that sweet smell of canvas and flowers, and it reminds me of how we proudly carried our gardens on a plate to be judged. My sister always beat me!

The week before the carnival, the Carnival Queen and two escorts were chosen. I used to love looking at the dresses that were displayed in the draper's shop that is now Nesta's. A procession through the village began the Carnival night and everyone joined in. The traffic was halted because the vehicles went both ways through the village then – imagine the chaos it would cause now with double-decker buses trying to get past the Somerfield Supermarket.

Talking of buses, there was just one to Weston, the No 20, and it started at the Bath Spa Station and went to the end of the village, as we called it. It cost one penny to the Memorial or 1½d to the end. I used to beg my father to let us travel to "The End" so that we could collect a green ticket! The penny ones were only white. Oh, if our dog travelled with us that was exciting because we had to sit upstairs with her and buy her a pink ticket. I collected lots of those tickets. I loved the 'ping' as the conductor punched them on a machine worn around the waist. The tickets were carried on a wooden board. You never hear a conductor say 'hold tight' now – well, there are no conductors are there?

I mentioned "The End" of the village, because to us children it was! Where Vernslade and Weston All Saints School is now was all fields and brambles, and it had lovely dips for riding bicycles up and down. By this time I had graduated to a "big" bike – a Hercules with 3 speeds. I thought I was the bees knees on this bike and hated getting it dirty, so I was very glad of the village brook to clean it off before going home.

The summers in those days seemed to go on and on, lovely warm days spent in the fields building dens, taking jam sandwiches out to eat as a picnic, and forming clubs! Though we spent so long making up rules for the club we never really had an actual club! We collected beads and kept them in little tobacco tins, and if you were lucky enough to get a Crystal, well, because mostly all we collected were jet – boring and not worth swapping.

Our parents never worried about us – we were all safe in those days and very few cars came into the Estate. We were quite safe holding long ropes across the road to see who could jump the highest.

Every year we were taken on holiday to Weymouth to stay for a whole week in a Caravan at Bowleaze Cove. I remember my father worked overtime for weeks to pay for this yearly treat. Oh, the excitement of going down to Green Park Station to watch the train come steaming in. I always marvelled at the way it always stopped about two inches before the buffers! I was so proud of my wooden spade or tin bucket, which of course was carried all the way to let people see I was going on holiday. I can still remember my blue knitted swimming costume.

Holidays and summer soon ends, though, and I had to go back to school. Oh, how I hated that Village School opposite the Post Office. Girls in one playground, boys in another! My teacher was Miss Parsons who was very old. We had to start each day chanting our 'times tables.' I was, and still am, hopeless at maths, and she used to keep me behind most days to 'get it right.' And oh, the milk – ugh! It was put in a huge saucepan and placed on the coke stove in the classroom, which was the only heat we had, to warm up – and it never did! When it was put in horrible plastic cups at playtime, it was lukewarm with skin on it! That has put me off warm milk for good. Another thing I shall never forget – the toilets. These were outside in the playground. In fact, the girls' toilet can still be seen today at the bottom of the steps leading to the girls' playground. Each class had their own toilet, and on cold days we didn't hang around there! The only nice thing I remember was on Friday afternoon, when we had a story read to us by Mr Pike the Headmaster. They were always the Adventure Stories by Enid Blyton. I loved Friday afternoons.

As I said, I hated that school. The crunch finally came when I again got my 'sums wrong' and the master called me out in front of the class and said that he would put me in a sack! And that it wouldn't be a Hossack (that was my surname). Unfortunately, at the same time as telling me off he was shaking a cane at me, and as he got more annoyed so the cane came nearer my face, and as he got to 'Hossack,' smack the cane went across my face, and as it was a split cane I was badly cut. He tried to stem the bleeding and kept saying, "Don't tell your mother," but I didn't have to – she saw the scar and thank goodness me and my sister were taken away from All Saints and sent to Newbridge St John's. That was great because we had to go on the bus! No tickets though unfortunately, we had to have a boring white bus pass.

Every Sunday we were sent to Church. Best coats on and off we went with our friends – all four of us! I can't remember anything about the services we attended except that it was called 'Matins' and all serious and sombre, but I do remember afterwards, because of having to put a penny in the collection. We were given a three penny bit to spend in 'Harrops' the sweet shop (this shop is now H R Electronics). Oh, the time we spent in that shop choosing our sweets – ½d chews, 1d liquorice. Mr Harrop was a very bad tempered man, very small, with glasses, and he really must have dreaded us coming into his shop!

Sunday afternoons I liked very much, because my sister and I went to Sunday School. I still remember Miss Hargood-Ash. She was a very old lady with a moustache and always wore knitted 'stockings'. Little did I know then how very knowledgeable she was – hence her books on the history of Weston Village. All I can remember is we had to repeat and repeat the Catechism! I liked the stories best, and a great incentive to go regularly to Sunday School was that every time you attended you were given a 'text'. These lovely pictures were stuck in books, which we kept and took home; I still have my bible that was given to me for good attendance. After Sunday School we always played on the handrail that leads up the slope to the church. We used to curl up and go over and over the rail, but all this came to a sudden end for me when I got too enthusiastic and ripped my new dress. Golly, I was frightened to go home!

I can remember a bit about the shops. I mentioned Harrops, the sweet shop. Down the side of this there were cottages (of course Greenbank Gardens were fields then) and Dallimores had a fruit shop there. The Cottage Gardens stretched to Gainsborough Court and this was then the Co-op. Every Monday, Ron would come to our house on his bicycle and take the order, and by Friday the groceries would be delivered. In the meantime, for any bits of extras we had to go to the Co-op – I still remember our numbers for the Dividend, 7213. I think the most exciting thing I remember was going to "town" shopping, and going into what is now the Pizza Hut. Then it was Bush's, a sort of huge grocery store, and they used the pulley system for payment. The assistant put the money into a small drum and twisted it closed, then fixed it to a hook on a rail above her head, and by pulling a lever sent it flying across the shop to the main Cash Desk. Here the money was counted and the change and receipt put in the drum and back it came. Much more fun than the card system we use now, and throughout that time my mother sat on a chair that was placed in front of the counters so that customers could shop comfortably. Then the purchases were all placed in a brown paper carrier bag with string handles.

Getting back to the village: the shop which is now the Insurance Company was the Co-op Butcher shop, and it was so busy there were nearly always queues out onto the pavement. Mind you, it was very small even in those days. The butcher was called Joe. Then there were two little cottages facing onto what is now the entrance to the Somerfield Car Park. There was a very pretty girl who lived in one of those cottages – she was a Carnival Queen once, and married a sailor. We used to love to catch a glimpse of him in his uniform! The original cottages are still by the side of the Post Office, which in those days was half grocery shop and a tiny Post Office, only then they were outside on the pavement!

Across the road by the Memorial was Mrs Chapples shop – a bakery (now a hairdressers). Oh, the delicious smells that came from there. Next door on the corner was the Manor Shop – a very nice sweet shop! The shop I remember with affection was up the hill where now is St Clements Court, this was a shoe repairer called Mr Trowbridge. It was a tiny shop and as you entered a large bell rang and out would come a dear old man with white hair and a black leather apron around his waist. There was a lovely smell of glue and leather in that shop. He was a very wily man because he used to put a notice in his window headed "These People Owe me Money!" And there were the names listed below: a clever idea, because it never stayed in the window very long!

I love Weston Village although it has changed so much now, but I am still proud to be on the BA1 side of the City!

The Pageant of Weston

The Festival of Britain was held in 1951.

In 1851, Prince Albert, Consort to Queen Victoria, felt that Britain's prowess in the fields of business, science and enterprise should be shown to the world and her achievements be celebrated. Now, 100 years later, the Nation again wanted to celebrate. The war was over, the future was full of hope and thanksgiving, and the people wanted to be festive after more than six years of anxiety and hardship.

In the little Somerset village of Weston, on the outskirts of Bath, the Vicar of the Parish Church of All Saints, the Reverend Everhard Rowe, called a meeting of all the organisations of the parish to discuss what celebrations could be held in the village. He suggested a Pageant of Weston, to be held on the recreation ground in the summer. But who was there to organise and write such an ambitious event? The newly formed Village Townswomen's Guild found the answer. One of their members, Mrs Begley, a historian, said she would compile the story after interviewing local people. Margaret Bodley, Chairman of the Guild, offered to do costumes and help with rehearsals, but she was a bit tied by the fact that her two sons were both under four. Dorothy Dix, the daughter of the Town Clerk of Bath, was appointed to coordinate and direct the whole event.

Weston at that time still had a strong sense of community, although the influx of people into the new houses spreading over the fields surrounding the village inevitably diluted this feeling. And 1951 was the year when Weston lost its identity – it was incorporated, by act of Parliament, into the City of Bath.

Members of both the Townswomen's Guilds in the village (morning and evening) entered into the venture of performing a pageant with enthusiasm. The older villagers were only too ready to divulge tales of the village in the past and Mrs Begley was inundated with stories.

They included the attempted drowning of a local woman in the stream that ran through the village because she had been seen out with a man on the day after her husband's funeral. She was saved by the Vicar of that time who came down and cut the rope dragging her along. I had verification of this event in about 1956, when an old man stopped outside my new house (built on what used to be the original recreation ground) where I was gardening and said how things had changed. He was visiting after an absence of many years and went on to talk about the 'old days'. He told me how, as a small boy, he had joined in the breaking down of a woman's door to drag her out to be put in the stream, and confirmed the story in every detail. Mrs Begley also heard all the details from those involved in the dismantling of 'The Firs', the Tudor house that was situated at the bottom of Lansdown Lane – then a real lane, as it still was in 1951. The owner, a single lady with a companion, had gone off in her horse and trap with her companion and had never returned. The villagers systematically removed everything including the house itself. We heard where the clocks had gone, the beams from the roof etc, and how the police did periodic raids on homes to see if there was any of the loot there. Because Weston was then such a rough place, the policemen had to go about in pairs, but they did not have much success in finding goods from The Firs. No boy from another village could come courting a Weston girl without risking being beaten up, which was verified by one of the TG members whose boyfriend had experienced this as late as 1930.

The day of the Pageant arrived and the narrator announced stories over the amplifier, and the scenes were enacted silently with an occasional remark from the actors.

The first scene was the building of the Via Julia, the Roman road through the village, the work being done by the Ancient Britons, the slaves of the conquering Romans; then the story of St Alphege, son of a Saxon woman in the village, who became Abbot of Bath and finally Archbishop of Canterbury; on to the Crusaders, then how Weston became the property of the Abbey of Bath for the next 400 years until the Dissolution of the Monasteries in 1539 when it passed to the Crown. After this came the Elizabethan times, the Civil War and the Battle of Lansdown; the visit of Queen Anne to Bath, the war against Napoleon which brought big prices and distress to the village with the women supporting their families at the washtub, when Weston was known as the Laundry of Bath.

Amid this poverty a charitable lady of the parish, Miss Resbery Hocker, started classes to teach the poor to read and write, and the nineteenth century saw many improvements to the village, with a school, sanitary drainage and better drinking water, mainly due to the efforts of Rev Bond, vicar of the parish for more than 50 years. Time passes and the scene shows the 1914-18 war with many men going to fight, followed by the rise of Hitler which affected men, women and children alike, the celebrations when Peace came, and finally the farewell to Weston as a separate village when it was incorporated into the City of Bath in 1951.

Weston Bowls Club

Club records show that a three rink green was laid on land owned by Miss Carr of Weston Manor at Penn Hill Road in 1930. Before that, bowling had taken place on the lawn of All Saints vicarage through the good offices of Rev. F A Bromley, who was to remain President of the club until his death in 1951.

In addition to Rev. Bromley, founder members of the club were Bill Blake, tobacconist in the village; Harry Cross, local builder; Don Pike, headmaster of the village school; and Alfred Stokes, groundsman. Alfred Stokes's son and daughter-in-law, Ray and Margaret Stokes, maintain the family tradition as keen bowlers and stalwarts of the club. Ray is a Past President and was Captain during the club's jubilee year in 1980. He is currently Vice-Captain and is often seen behind the bar in the clubhouse.

In 1937, the green was extended to six rinks at a cost of £646 7s 8d. Miss Carr contributed £450 as a loan and was paid an annual rent of £2 – £1 to be paid on 25th March and £1 on 29th September. A lease was drawn up on 26th October 1937 for bowling to take place on this land for 60 years, expiring on 29th September 1997. In 1946 Miss Carr cancelled her outstanding loan and the following year sold the land to the Parochial Church Council, subject to the lease, for £50. Two years later Rev. Bromley negotiated the purchase of extra land, at that time being farmed by tenant Mr. Chubb. Rev. Bromley paid £53 to the Parochial Church Council for an eighth of an acre, and the club paid 5s 0d per annum for the lease, on the same terms as the original.

It was not until 1972 that plans were drawn up to erect a Prattens prefabricated building to provide a new pavilion and bar, costing between £3,000 and £6,000, depending on the amount of work undertaken by members. This, however, would have meant a loss of parking facilities, and was rejected by Bath City Council. As a result, the club negotiated the lease of some extra land for 15 years at a cost of £15 per year. Unfortunately, due to these delays the cost of the Prattens building had risen to £11,000, which was beyond the club's means. So members came to the conclusion that they had no choice but to extend the existing pavilion and tore up the lease for the extra land which they would no longer need.

In 1984, four years after celebrating its Golden Jubilee, the club approached the Diocese of Bath & Wells to buy the land outright. The Diocese put a value of £40,000 on it; however, some clever negotiating by club members reduced this to £18,000, provided that a covenant was drawn up that the land must always remain a sports facility should it ever be put on the open market for sale. A tremendous amount of fund raising had to be undertaken in order to raise this amount, but it was achieved and as a result the club is now independent and it is generally accepted that Weston has the best green in the area.

The club has flourished over the years and has a maximum male membership of 90 with ages ranging from 20s to 80s – thanks to television coverage, bowling is no longer considered a game to take up when you retire.

Probably the greatest change in its history was the opening of the Ladies Section in 1997, which is allowed to have no more than one third of the men's membership. This move was not to the liking of everyone in the club, but the first season progressed well and I think some of the more sceptical members are coming round to the idea that the women are an asset, especially when it comes to the tea rota! In 1998, occasional mixed bowling was introduced, and as there are quite a number of husband and wife players it is hoped that this will develop. Weston Village TG member Gillian Lillicrap was the first Captain of the Ladies Section with Margaret Stokes, wife of the aforementioned Ray, taking over in 1998.

New moves are now afoot to provide better clubhouse and changing facilities, which would include indoor short-mat bowling. Plans were drawn up and a submission made to the Lottery Commissioners for a grant towards the projected cost of £240,000. Unfortunately, this was unsuccessful, so the decision was made to go for a self-build scheme in order to keep costs down. This is now under way – the steel framework of the new clubhouse having been erected during the summer of 1999.

It is hoped that the improved facilities will prove to be a great asset to the village and attract more members to what is a very friendly and congenial sporting and social amenity. New bowlers will be warmly welcomed, especially by David Burton, English Bowling Association Coach and Weston Club Coach, who will be delighted to point them in the right direction.

As a new member of the Ladies Section, I have to warn you that it is not always blue sky and immaculate lawns. I shall never forget my first attempt at bowling in May 1997 when the hailstones came down so thick that the white jacks were buried! However, when the sun is shining it is most pleasant and I have found my fellow bowlers so generous in their encouragement and help.

In conclusion, let us have a look at some of the club's notable achievements. Its most famous player was Sid Bond, who was an England Trialist. In 1955, 1975 and 1978 the club was runner-up in the Florence

Morris Trophy. Then there was a lull until 1998, when the club was delighted to win the Turnbull Cup. In 1999 they finished top of the new Somerset Premier League, were runners-up in the Second Division and won the Midsomerset League. All these competitions are organised by Somerset County Bowling Association and the results are a great encouragement to members.

Club tours were started in 1991 to Torquay and we hope to bowl in Spain in the year 2000. Is this the Armada in reverse?

Weston Billiards Club

Weston Billiards Club was founded in 1862 in Church Street by the curate of the parish and was known as Weston Working Mens Club and Reading Room. Rev. Bond decided to rebuild the rooms in 1873 at a cost of £500. The front downstairs room was kept for the Vicar's exclusive use, while upstairs the men had a room where they could play draughts, dominoes, chess and bagatelle. In 1892, Mrs Frazer donated a three-quarter size billiard table, and some years later a full size table was added.

Bath Billiards and Snooker League was formed in 1920 and the Weston Club was a founder member, and is the only club to have had continuous membership since its inception. In the early days fees were £5 for honorary members and 4 shillings for ordinary members, payable by 1 shilling per quarter, which is laid down in the Deeds.

The Club has Trustees and is run by a committee, of which the Vicar was always Chairman. The current Chairman is Mr. R. Bowden, one of the longest serving members and a former secretary of the club from 1933-52. The Club's current membership stands at 70.

In the early fifties the Club was approached by Bath Library with a view to renting the downstairs back room as a lending library for the village. This was agreed and was so successful that the Vicar agreed to give up the front room so that the library could spread into this room to meet increasing demands from the village. They have continued to rent both downstairs rooms ever since, although cutbacks in funding have reduced the opening times for the library.

Weston Billiards Club continues to use the first floor as before and is financially self-sufficient, the rent from the library helping towards the maintenance of the building.

More Memories of War

On the morning of Thursday August 31st 1939, I travelled to work as usual, catching the No.65 bus from Ealing Broadway, to the Ministry of Labour at Kew, where I had worked since leaving school at seventeen years old.

Of course, at this time everyone was aware that only a miracle could avert war with Germany. Buildings of importance were sandbagged, and the public informed as to air raid precautions. As early as 1938, when Mr Chamberlain met Hitler at Munich, a huge trench was dug in Hyde Park, in readiness for a public shelter.

The crisis was of such long standing, that on this sunny summer morning miracles seemed possible, and my little world secure. A friend and I had tickets for a play in the West End for that very evening.

It was not to be. By mid-afternoon I, who had never been away from home on my own before, was sitting, hot and apprehensive, in a train bound for Bath, to help cope with the planned evacuation of mothers and children from London. War had become very real. Inside my suspender belt, pinned on for safety, was a £5 note (printed on Indian paper – very large and impressive). This was an imprest issued to junior Civil Servants, and only to be spent in an emergency.

I arrived at Bath's Labour Exchange – the bomb-scarred remains of which still stand at the corner of Milk Street – at about 6.30pm. The office was closed by then, of course. Ringing the bell seemed futile, but, in desperation, I did. Fortunately, the typist and the Manager were still in the building. The young woman had committed the cardinal sin of not reporting her marriage. Marriage in those days forfeited a woman's rights to permanent status and a pension in the Civil Service. Her job was on the line. My frantic ringing and banging interrupted the proceedings, and I was admitted by a red-eyed girl and taken to an equally red-faced gentleman sitting behind a large desk.

I was not expected. Many Labour Exchanges had not finalised arrangements to accommodate the influx of staff from headquarters. My arrival took the heat out of the situation. The urgency of where I was to be housed took precedence over the typist's predicament, at least for the time being. Despite her own distress, and to the Manager's embarrassed gratitude, this kind girl solved the problem by taking me to her sister-in-law in Penn Lea Road, Weston. This lady had reluctantly agreed to accept two evacuated bank clerks, but to my relief preferred to house females. I was made very welcome.

The next day another girl from Kew, Doris, turned up at the Exchange. She had arrived in Bath even later than I, and after being mercilessly grilled by some dragon of a woman at the YWCA as to her credentials, had spent the night there, most of it in tears. After consultation with the typist, Doris came back to my billet and was thankfully accepted by my kind hostess as her second contribution to the war effort. At first I was very homesick, although I found Bath very beautiful – a honey coloured city, set in the hollow of surrounding green hills.

Then, just as I was beginning to enjoy a newly found freedom my parents were posted by the Admiralty to Bath. In the early spring of 1940 we moved into a newly built house in Broadmoor Vale, next door to the builder, Arthur Mortimer, who, many years later, became Mayor of Bath. Part of me was glad to resume family life, and I transferred from the Ministry of Labour to the Admiralty, in order to stay in Bath. The cold war had dragged on, and lulled into a sense of false security, the evacuees were drifting back to London. I was due to be posted back. Life in a hostel seemed bleak in contrast to my cosy home. I had reckoned without the drawbacks.

My social life had continued to improve. A club had been formed for civil servants. There were dances at the Pump Room – how that lovely sprung floor vibrated under boots not meant for dancing!

All these functions ended very respectably at 10pm, in time for last buses. But buses stopped running when the air raid sirens sounded. This happened all too frequently, because although Bath mainly escaped the attention of the Luftwaffe until the two ghastly nights of April 25th and 26th 1942, Bristol was devastated regularly and tragically.

It is a long and time-consuming walk from the centre of Bath to Broadmoor Vale, and my mother, never in the best of health, worried desperately if I failed to be indoors by ten-thirty. It has to be borne in mind that the drone of aircraft overhead was unnerving. The thud of bombs seemed very close across the intervening hills, and the sky glowed red over Bristol's inferno. Consequently, my late homecoming caused some friction. I felt guilty and resentful; I am sure my parents did also. Taken in context with the horrors of war, such small problems are insignificant, but when you are young they loom large.

On one such occasion, I flounced off to bed, and in defiance of the blackout regulations, left my window open and un-blacked out, undressing in the dark. It was very warm that summer, but the night air from the slopes of Lansdown tempered the heat. It also cooled my resentment at what seemed an unreasonable curtailment of my freedom. Full of self-pity, I sat on the bed rubbing the cramped muscles in my legs. I had always suffered from rheumatism, and my high-heeled shoes were hardly suitable for hiking, especially after an evening's dancing. Careful to avoid another spasm, I slipped between the sheets. I was just drifting off to sleep when the drone of a solitary plane, flying very low, woke me. Then came an almighty thud, which shook the house, rattling my open windows.

A homeward bound German pilot was unloading his surplus bombs at random. One had exploded in the open fields behind Broadmoor Vale. The excruciating pain of another attack of cramp not only outweighed my abject terror, but also reassured me that I was still alive. Of course, I did not dare switch on the light, but groped my way into the bathroom to get my liniment.

On the way, I collided with my parents, and was in further trouble on account of my un-blacked out bedroom. However, a sense of proportion had been restored all round. I sat on the edge of my bed, once more rubbing my feet and legs, blissfully glad to be alive, and aware of a pleasant fragrance in the night air. It was not until the next morning that I discovered that the bottle on the floor contained lavatory cleaner. My liniment was still on the shelf in the bathroom.

Reminiscences of Childhood in the 1930s

Here is a selection of reminiscences and anecdotes from various residents of Weston, mostly as they were written for us.

I remember some of my early days at Weston school. The girl's playground was on the left and the boys on the right. I can even see to this day Miss Frayling arriving on her large very upright bicycle.

When it was lunch break at ten to eleven, some of the children would call over the school wall to Mrs Gillard who had the newsagents and sweet shop opposite – "Mrs Gillard, halfpenny worth of broken up toffee please," or sweethearts which were sugar sweets with 'I love you' and things like that written on them, or liquorice etc, and Mrs Gillard would bring them across the road and hand them up over the wall and collect the half pennies.

We had the baker's shop opposite and on my first day at the 'big' school as we called it, my mother brought my mid-morning lunch over to me and Mr Pike saw this and from then on I was privileged to go home for ten minutes so that my mother did not have to leave the shop. This meant I had to go down the slipway by the boy's playground.

There was a little shop on the corner of Lansdown Place and Crown Hill, on the steps, with its stone floor, owned by Miss Williams who was an elderly old-fashioned lady who wore long black skirts. I also recall the butchers shop in the High Street, and sometimes when customers were in the shop buying their meat, the animals would arrive and were brought through the shop to the slaughterhouse at the rear.

I remember the cows from Chubb's farm, now Greenbank Gardens, coming from the farm every day after milking and being driven across the road by the War Memorial and up Crown Hill to the field (now Lucklands) for grazing, and returning later in the day for the second milking.

On race days a lot of people would arrive by tramcar at the terminus by the War Memorial and school and walk through the village to Lansdown for the races, and back again for the return journey, some happy and some not so happy.

Miss Smith ran the ironmongers where the Crown Hill flats are now. The shop smelt of paraffin. She gave piano lessons upstairs. Miss Little ran a small grocery shop on the corner of Manor Road and Lansdown Place. Newmans had a hardware shop where Nesta's the hairdressers is now. Jonquils was where the Simmons's sold home made ice cream at ½d a cornet, lovely!

Tucker's grocery was a post office as well.

Elsie Young opened a cold meat shop (Jonquils now) after Young's butchers closed. Mrs Brooks had a faggots and peas shop where the Coffee Mill is now. Also Miss Hanson had a wool shop there. Dyers had a fish and chip shop near Davis's dairy.

One of the characters of the village was Lionel Smith who delivered papers to houses in Weston Park. He wore a cap always and had no teeth. He walked to the Methodist Church at the top of Chelsea Road twice every Sunday. His sister, Miss Smith, kept the hardware shop.

Miss Parson (teacher) always wore a green 2 piece and her hair was plaited and worn in 'ear phones'. As she walked up and down the aisles in class the children used to lift the back of her jacket with a ruler or pencil!

Another character was a man called Mr Williams-Lear who lived opposite Shergold's farm!

There was a water tank in the fields where Lucklands are now. One day a little girl was showing her friends how to tap dance on the top of it when she fell in. They were all frightened to go home because she was soaking wet!

Ern and Gwen Fletcher at Fletchers Farm (to the right of Perry's), delivered milk to the village in a large churn from a horse and cart and later in a motorbike and side car. Gwen used to carry the large churns! You brought your jugs to the door for the milk to be ladled into.

Hiskens bakers shop, to start with had a tearoom on the left side of the shop and bakers and confectionery on right side. Later on, the tearoom closed and greengrocery was sold instead. You could get seven currant buns for 6d. A small loaf was 1¾d, a 2lb loaf was 2¾d. Hiskens were well known for their custard slices. A Mr Gaynor used to come every Saturday in a chauffeur driven car to buy custard slices.

Children used to play marbles in the gutter in Manor Road, and also played with hoops, whips and tops. Also hopscotch.

Sunday school and church in morning. Then when older went onto bible class.

There was also something called the 'King's Messengers' run by Miss Stallard. You knitted and read.

At the top end of the village was the Globe Inn pub. It was so small they called it "the matchbox". The landlords were the Smith brothers. Across the road was Bill Blake's sweet shop, coming down through the village were Mortimer's building and joinery yard, then Shergold's farm, the open brook, opposite was Dyer's fish and chip shop, the Crown and Anchor pub, landlord Mr Francome. Opposite Harry Webb's coffee shop, Charlie Dolman's all sorts shop, the King's Head pub, the hardware shop. Infant school, Harold's sweetshop, Young's the butcher and slaughterman, Tucker groceries, Gillard's paper shop, senior school, Hiskin's bread and cake shop, Jones' the dairy, Bond the coalman. Harry Webb's coffee shop charged accumulators and batteries for radios.

At Charlie Dolman's shop you could buy such things as bacon, eggs, cheese, rabbit, pheasant and there was always a cat or two sat in the window.

The village consisted mainly of large families like the Pitmans, she used to make faggots and sell them. Then the Shepherds, the Smiths, the Richards, the Crosses. The Paines, the Kimbers, the Webbs, the Burfords, the Mortimers, the Stokes.

At Crown Hill we had the forgery for ironwork and shodding the horses, also George Trowbridge shoe repairs, he used to collect and deliver the shoes on his bicycle.

There used to be an alleyway at the right hand side of the Crown and Anchor pub. It was an entrance to a row of old cottages and it was called "Cockles Alley" – the residents called it "pigs eye view", because the pigs looked into the back window.

Before the war the village had its own football team and fire brigade, who practised using water from the brook, which was very exciting to watch. We didn't have television or radio but we had a lot of entertainment with concerts and dances in the church room, or in fine weather we danced in the street or on the old recreation ground with the All Saints Village Band which was led by Walter Bray and was very good.

It was a sad day for Weston councillors when it was decided that Weston should be amalgamated with Bath. After takeover the parish council was almost powerless, and the last chairman, Mr W Blake, asked all his council members to attend a special service at All Saints Church, and the Mayor of Bath shook hands with Mr Blake as a sign that power had been handed over in a friendly manner.

How the Shops Have Changed

In 1993 the Sartain sisters were interviewed – Elsie, now Mrs Ferris, aged 85, and Alice aged 94. They were born and bred in Weston village, their mother having been brought up in Primrose Hill. Their father was born in Bristol but settled in Weston when he married. Mr and Mrs Sartain produced seventeen children of which ten survived. They told with great glee of their recollections from their childhood days in the village – like the day when Mr Young the butcher's cows, awaiting slaughter in the back yard behind his shop, got out and ate all the flowers in their neighbour's front garden!

Here is a list of present buildings and shops and what they used to be during the early part of this century when the Sartain family was young, starting in the vicinity of the War Memorial:

Weston Garages – Greenings Garages

Manor Dental Surgery, Manor Rd – Day's Dairy, and in later years Williams' Grocery.

Manor Road – Weston Fire Brigade, who had their own band.

New Edition Hairdressers – Hiskins' Bakery.

Weston Pet Shop – Williams Drapers, the only shop where Mrs Sartain Snr could buy an extra long hatpin to accommodate her luxuriant hair, at a cost of 1 penny.

Crown Hill Flats – Mr Holcombe, blacksmith; Mr Trowbridge, cobbler, who used to display a list of debtors in his shop window; Mr Smith's ironmongery.

Chaplins Newsagents – Gillard's paper shop.

Post Office – Tuckers Grocery.

Bath Insurance & Mortgage Co. – Young's Butchers Shop, which moved to Trafalgar Rd (see Jonquils below). It was here that he kept his cattle in the back yard, having walked them through the shop, ready for slaughter!

HR Electronics – Dolman's Grocery with Harold's Sweet Shop next door.

Maison Nesta – Drapers

Scout Hall – School divided into three sections: babies (mixed), junior boys and junior girls.

Library – Reading Rooms.

Large House at church end of Church Street – Private school for young ladies.

New flats at top of Trafalgar Road – Pointings Brewery and later Carpenters Nursery. There was also a fruit and vegetable shop just around the corner (later run by John Brain in the sixties), which is now an attractive house. Almost opposite this house was a brewery.

Jonquils Flower Shop – Queen's Head pub with yet another brewery! They were a thirsty lot in Weston in those days. Later became Young's Butchers Shop with slaughterhouse behind. It was not necessary to drive the animals through the shop here as there was a wide, arched entrance in Trafalgar Road leading to a large yard containing a well.

Panda Fish Bar – Bonds Bakery and Weston Weighbridge – the grill is still visible in the wall.

Sheppards Gardens –Tuckers Grocery, run by a relation of the one in the High Street (now the Post Office); Shergoods Chapel, which had its own band that played outside each Sunday at 6pm; Young's Coaches (relation of the butcher), which was approached through an archway – they had old Bedfords with wooden slatted seats! Above was the coffin maker. This complex later became Mortimer's Builders Yard.

Weston Card Shop – Mrs Moons Coffee Shop, which was a favourite haunt of bikers from Bristol, who drove in via Penn Lea Road – an early version of the 60s rockers? They were apparently very fond of her homemade cakes and biscuits!

82 High Street – The Globe pub, the smallest in the city.

Drinking water was available from the pump opposite the Kings Head Pub, which is still there. In their young days the Sartain family lived in one of the cottages opposite the school (now a row of modern shops – bookmaker, hairdresser, greengrocer). Every drop of water they needed – and remember there were ten children in the family plus mother and father – had to be carried from this pump. It was here that the neighbour's flowers were eaten by Mr Young's cows.

Weston Village Street Names

After the First World War new estates quickly grew up on the upper slopes of the village bringing new families into the area. The streets were well laid out and gardens soon became a feature of the new houses. To honour some of Bath's well known men who had been residents of old Weston and who are buried in All Saints churchyard, many of the new streets were named after them.

Here are a selection of street names and their origins:

Duncan Gardens

Called after John Shute Duncan and Philip Bury Duncan, who lived in Weston Road, and have a monument in All Saints Church. The brothers, who lived together, gave great service to literature and science in Bath.

Philip came to Bath from Oxford where he was Resident Fellow of New College, and Curator of the Ashmolean Museum. His services to the University were acknowledged by the diploma of LLD. The knowledge and experience gained at Oxford were of great value in the work of forming a high class Library at the Bath Royal Literary and Scientific Institution of which he was one of the most prominent founders, and also in founding a local museum.

He gave evening lectures at the Institution on a great variety of subjects, for example: Painting, Sculpture, Botany, Zoology, Geology, Foreign Travel, Quackery, The Voice of Birds, Conversation, Novels, The Nature of Human Hair, and A Gentleman's Day in Ancient Rome, when the lecture hall was always well filled. His varied ability, liberal disposition and quiet generosity were much admired. He was helped in every way by his "excellent brother".

The brothers were especially interested in the preservation and arrangement of the Roman remains found at various times in Bath, and to commemorate this and other services, a brass plate was affixed in the vestibule of the Bath Royal Literary and Scientific Institution, surmounted by two portraits in the same frame, presented by the daughter of Mr J S Duncan, Mrs Fraser, late of Manchester. As a small tribute to their memories, £500 was subscribed in various parts of the kingdom and vested in trust for the promotion of the Library and Museum, to which they were especially devoted.

Falconer Road

Called after one or more of the three Dr Falconers, who were doctors in the eighteenth century. It is remarkable that father, son and grandson succeeded each other at Bath in the medical profession. The family was of Caledonian origin, its genealogical head being Sir Alexander Falconer, a Lord of Sessions in 1639.

The first Dr Falconer was the son of the Recorder of Chester, where he was born in 1744. The Recorder became a Freeman of Chester in 1733, and all the male representatives of the family were successively admitted to the privilege.

The first Dr Falconer settled in Bath in 1770 at No 29 The Circus, was admitted as a fellow of the Royal Society in 1773, and became physician to the Mineral Water Hospital in 1734. He wrote 47 books, many on medical subjects, the classics, theology, botany and natural history, the latter including papers for two societies in which he took great interest – The Bath and West of England Literary and Philosophical Society, and the Manchester Literary and Philosophical Society.

His books on the Bath waters were held in high repute. The third edition of an "Essay on the influence of the passions on the Disorders of the Body", published in 1796, was given the first Forthergilian Gold Medal. The Medical Society of London gave its Silver Medal for "The Disease of the Hip Joint, and on the use of the Bath Waters as a remedy", published in 1805.

The high opinion of him by his brethren in the Metropolis led to his being consulted by a large number of distinguished people who came to Bath, among them Mr Pitt, whom he attended in Bath in his last illness in 1805. Dr Falconer died at his home in the Circus in 1824.

The second Dr Falconer, his son Thomas, also lived at 29 The Circus. After graduating at Oxford in 1810 as a Student for the Church, he filled the post of Bampton lecturer. He wrote twenty-three works, classical, medical and theological.

As a clergyman he assisted his friend the Rev. Richard Warner, the Bath historian, in his clerical work in St James's parish. After receiving the degree of MD, he gave much medical advice to the poor. He has been justly described as "a man of singular independence of character, a fine scholar and a notable citizen". He had five sons and two daughters. He died in 1839.

His son Randle Wilbraham was the third Dr Falconer. He was twice elected Mayor, a humane and judicious magistrate, a physician advancing the best interests of the profession both by his pen and practice, a supporter of numerous useful institutions, and established the Bath City lectures. He died in 1881.

Frankland Close

Named after Sir Charles Henry Frankland (Lord), born in 1716, who was Consul General in Lisbon for many years, and is buried in All Saints Churchyard (Tomb 113 by the lichgate leading to Lynfield Park). There is also a memorial tablet to him in the Church.

The developers of the estate had their original name "Haymead Way" turned down by the Council, who asked for a more suitable name.

Lord Frankland went to Massachusetts, North America, where he met and married a serving girl, whom he brought back to England. When he died in 1768 it was she who erected the tablet to his memory.

Haviland Grove and Haviland Park

After the Haviland family. There are tombs in the churchyard dating from James Haviland, who died in December 1779, to the last recorded member of the family to be buried there, who died in July 1852.

Holcombe Green

"Combe" is a valley. The opportunity arose to revive "Holcombe" by giving it to the houses built on the field still bearing this name. The local councillors declined to do this as "they did not want to be reminded of the past." Bath City Council thought differently and named their estate "Holcombe Green".

Lansdown Lane

"Lan" means an open space and "Dun" a fortified hill. It was originally called "Tibbots Lane", but changed its name after being widened to accommodate the visit of Queen Anne in the seventeenth century. It is said she was met by twenty-four maidens dressed in green in Weston Lane.

Lucklands Road

According to early maps this was the name of a farm. Water was piped from a stream running through the farmlands to Abbey Grange (now the Physiotherapy School).

Mortimer Close

After Edward W A Mortimer, affectionately known as "Arthur", who lived in Weston all his life. His father started a builders business in a small shed behind No 9 Trafalgar Road. His own yard was off Wellington Buildings, on the site of what is now Sheppards Gardens in the High Street. His firm was eventually taken over by Beazer.

He became successful and well known, being popular in both social and business circles in the City. He joined Kitcheners Army Volunteer RE, and saw service in France. He was Chairman and Life Member of Weston ex-Services Association. He was a keen sportsman, belonging to Weston Bowls Club and Bath Cycling Club. He was Chairman of Bath City Football Club. During his 30th years association with the Club, he urged help with finances. He was known as "Mr Bath City".

He entered the Council in 1951 for the Weston Ward, and was known for his wise counsel and sound judgement. He was the 731st Mayor in 1959 and left the Council in 1964.

He always showed concern for the safety and well-being of his neighbours in Broadmoor Vale. In the early days of the war he mobilised willing helpers to build an air-raid shelter in the field at the back of the Vale.

Purlewent Drive

Named after Samuel Purlewent, an eccentric 18th century Bath attorney, who is buried in All Saints Churchyard. He was an ardent Freeman of the City who worked and schemed to have the Commons, now Victoria Park and High Common (Approach Golf Course) leased to builders. He died in July 1792.

An extract from his will reads:-

> "It is my express will and desire that I may be buried at Weston in the County of Somerset, if I die there, if not to be carried down there (but not in a hearse) ... and when I arrive there I direct six poor people of Weston do support my corpse to the grave, and that I may be buried at twelve at noon, and that each of them do have half-a-guinea: and I hereby order and direct that a good boiled ham, a dozen fowls, a sirloin of beef, with plum puddings, may be provided at The Crown, in Weston, for the said eighteen poor people, besides the clerk and sexton. And I allow five guineas for the same: and I request and hope they will be as merry and cheerful as possible ... I desire that after I am buried there will be a cold collation provided at the public house, a sirloin of beef, potatoes, and a fillet of veal with plenty of good ale, where I hope they will refresh themselves with decency and propriety. No friends or relations whatever to attend my funeral."
>
> S. Purlewent, died July 30th 1792.

The Macies

Named after a family who were first mentioned in records of Weston in 1544, when John Macie, a Widcombe weaver had his goods assessed at £24 (a large sum then) on the subsidy roll.

In 1541 when Clement Eryngton resigned, another John Macie became Vicar. This John was an educated man with a BA degree. He came to Weston at the time of the Reformation.

In 1549 clerical marriages were legalised, and John married Eysot Wilcher, and they had five children. With the accession of Mary Tudor, clerical marriages were no longer allowed, and John was given time to divorce his wife, which he refused to do, and in 1554 he was deprived of his living. Usually another priest was appointed, but the living at Weston was left vacant until the end of Mary's reign. There are no records of baptisms or weddings in the registers. Nothing is known of those years, whether any services were performed elsewhere in the village, whether the church was closed, or how John and his family lived.

Under Elizabeth, John was reinstated. John and Eysot had two children before being deprived of his living, one before reinstatement, and two after returning to the Vicarage. One of the sons became "a Parson at Walcot". Eysot died in 1594 and John died in 1595.

The Macie family prospered during the next century. In the terrier (a book recording the site and boundaries of the land of private persons) of 1605, a John Macie held about 30 acres, and a Thomas Macie about 10 acres of land. Their social status rose, and they were granted a Coat of Arms and crest. They almost certainly lived at Weston House, which was probably rebuilt by some member of the family in the early 18th century.

In 1698 a David Macie became Vicar. Two years later he married Amie, daughter of John Harrington of Kelston. John Harrington held the Weston Rectoral tithes, which he gave to Weston in 1699 to augment the Vicar's stipend. Sadly David died in 1701, only three years after coming to the Vicarage. £120 left by Thomas Macie for the "second poor" of the Parish is now merged in the Weston Charities.

Drama and Music

After the success of the Pageant of Weston in 1951 the vicar of All Saints, Rev. Everhard Rowe and his wife, Margot, encouraged drama in the village and it was continued in the form of religious productions in the church. At Christmas of that year, the Coventry Nativity Play was performed in the church, followed by a Nativity play in mime and music the following year. This all fired the histrionic ambitions of quite a few of the local people, especially the young, and in 1957 a Children's Drama Group was formed by Margaret Bodley and Marjorie Eales when they presented the pantomime, "The Golden Goose".

When the village school vacated their old premises for the fine modern building in Broadmoor Lane, the church took over the present church centre, but it was obvious much work would be needed to make it suitable for functions and plays. A working party was formed with Rev. Rowe, Charles and Primrose Sawyers, Arthur and Margaret Bodley and Edwin White, augmented by John Osborne, Michael Messer and other helpers from time to time. Local builder, Mr Arthur Mortimer, and Mr Podger, provided help with the stage. Money for curtains and lights came from a performance of the pantomime "Cinderella" by the Children's Drama Group, written by Margaret Bodley. After that there was no holding back the aspiring actors and actresses.

As the young people grew out of belonging to a Children's Group, the All Saint's Drama Group was formed. Their first performance took place in October 1959 with a production of "Miss Quid's Plays Portia" together with a play by the Church Youth Club. The following year saw many excellent productions and a large number of villagers were involved. The play "Breath of Spring" brought the ASDG a taste of fame as it was entered for a drama festival and won a banner. Margaret Bodley and Sheila Barnsdale played the parts of two eccentric old ladies, and Ena Farson was the maid.

Although under the auspices of All Saints Church, membership of the Drama Group was open to people from other denominations, but this policy provoked disapproval from some church members. The group was called upon to justify its continued connection with the church. Sadly the day came when the All Saints Drama Group ceased to exist, but all was not lost as some of those who had played an important part in the ASDG were also associated with another drama group, that belonging to the Weston Village Townswomen's Guild. The producer for the group is Sheila Barnsdale, who is also a very clever playwright who writes her plays to suit the members of the group, several of which have been published for other groups to perform. Here she tells in her own words about the Guild's drama group.

The Drama Group

Anyone who has read the history of the Townswomen's Guild movement will know that Drama has always played an important part in group activities, and very high standards have been achieved in past years. When I joined the Weston TG in about 1957, there was a very active group which had been in existence, as far as I can ascertain, since the Guild was formed in the 1940s.

We had great fun rehearsing weekly at the Parish Hall, and in producing sketches and light entertainment as part of the year's programme, which included talks and slide shows on topics of interest by invited speakers at the Guild meetings. One amongst many sketches, entitled "Alright on the Night" I remember as being particularly hilarious. Despite the inevitable pre-performance nerves, I think the cast enjoyed it as much as the audience!

We gradually progressed to more ambitious work, and aimed to perform three-act plays, which provided more than post-business entertainment at meetings. This of course, required more time and dedication, and full evening performances.

We became aware that we had a lot to learn about all aspects of Drama, and decided that our subscriptions, together with the Guild funding allotted to Group activities, would cover help from a professional producer. This worked well, and we profited by the experience, but eventually the committee decided that it was too great a drain on the Guild resources, which in those days were not large. Not to be defeated we applied for help from the Theatre Guild, and a grant was approved, provided that our numbers did not fall below twelve members.

This excellent arrangement continued for a considerable period. Under the tuition of a succession of talented producers, we entered, as a group and individually, in the Mid-Somerset Festival. Excellent performances were given and won acclaim in this and several other festivals over the years. One of our members, Iris Kilburn, won the award of 'Best Actress of the Year', in one such competition. It was a performance of 'The Rag Woman', which is well remembered by us to this day.

As part of the Guild's charity supporting efforts, the Drama Group's annual programmes have included entertaining various clubs for the elderly and handicapped. In this field, we made many contacts, and were asked back on an annual basis. We received much pleasure, and hope we gave some, over many years. The hospitality shown on many of these occasions has been overwhelming. Eventually, unfortunately, our membership just failed to qualify for the grant from the Theatre Guild, and we had to sink or swim on our own.

Luckily, we had acquired enough knowledge of stage craft and production to get by, and it was now that Iris Kilburn bravely took on the task of producer. She made a great success of it, with humour and patience, not to mention the firmness needed in such a democratic bunch of women!

We had the satisfaction of creating sets, with flats borrowed from the All Saints Church Drama Group, and help enlisted from long-suffering husbands to build and dismantle them. We performed in the Church Hall as it was then called, in the excellent stage room adapted by early members of the Church Group, and the vicar, Rev. Rowe, until that drama group, of which I was also a member, was forced to disband. Consequently, the flats and costumes, which had been such a godsend to us, were disposed of due to lack of storage space.

We put on one or two performances using curtain sets, but since then have performed, mainly, in the Parish Hall, and managed to maintain as high a standard as possible, with considerably limited resources. It is surprising how a measure of adversity brings out hidden talent and ingenuity with amazingly good results!

Over the years it has become increasingly difficult to find plays for women which are suitable for casting. Many very good plays contain parts for younger women than our group can now provide. In addition to this difficulty, owing to ill health, our producer, Iris, can no longer do more than act in an advisory capacity, which she still does. They say "fools step in where angels fear to tread", so proving this to be true I have stepped into Iris's shoes, and am producing whatever plays we can find, supplemented by some I have had the temerity to write myself.

Some years ago, an excerpt from one three act play called 'A House of Women' was entered in a Drama Festival in Cardiff for Townswomen's Guild drama groups. The play was set in the Victorian era, and with the help of Margaret Bodley, who is a member of the Costume Society, and who organised and instructed us, our dress was correct in every detail to pass inspection of adjudication. We hired a mini-bus, to be driven by an intrepid member of the cast, and, laden with costumes and furniture, including a fireplace hired from Walcot Reclamation Centre, we set off one bitterly cold morning.

After a hasty lunch on arrival, we had to comply with the rules of the competition by setting the stage to a given time, performing, also within strict time limits, then striking set, also to a given time. Despite not achieving top place, we had a very creditable adjudication, and Min Stephens, our President, was commended on her 'cameo performance' as the elderly parlour maid, and friend of the family. We arrived back in Weston, happy but worn out by all our exertions. All credit due to the driver of the mini-bus, who had a considerable part to play, both on and off stage.

So, we continue to play our parts, still enjoying our Drama activities within a closely knit group.

The Choir

Another form of entertainment much enjoyed by Guild members is music, and just as they are fortunate in having their own playwright they also had until recently their own composer. This was Iris Gardener, who with Margaret Friend (mezzo soprano), Jane Croft and Maureen Bannock (both sopranos) and Iris's contralto voice, arranged concerts for charity, many times singing Iris's own compositions. Iris was also the Guild's pianist and an enthusiastic member of the Guild's choir, which over the years has raised considerable sums for various local charities and visits old people's homes for concerts. Lee Truman is the current conductor and several of Iris's songs have been included in the choir's repertoire.

The Guild now boasts a group called the "Songsters" who sing selections of light music to various groups in the Bath area.

Parade Gardens, Bath, 1999

A Community Centre for the Millennium

With the increase in housing and the growth of the population of Weston the need for a larger Community Centre has long been realised – but the village itself is not elastic and it seemed that there was no available space for such a building. The Church Centre in the High Street has served the village people well, but the small space does get rather crowded on occasions, so what was the answer?

A Community Centre needs to be in a central position with easy access, it should provide space for various events from meetings to plays and concerts, from playgroups to ballroom dancing, discussions to sports, flower shows to film shows, all for some 300 people.

A solution to the problem was discussed at a meeting in January 1997, when plans to develop the Church Centre were announced by the Rector of All Saints Church, Rev. Patrick Whitworth, and received a warm reception from more than one hundred residents present.

All Saints Church owns the site and the building, a grade two listed building which was set up in 1845 in trust to further the education of both adults and children. The school left the building in 1961, and since then it has been the nearest thing to a community centre that we have in Weston.

The plan is to leave the present front aspect of the old building as it is, and to build new buildings onto the back section giving ample space for all the village needs. Planning permission has been approved and sufficient money raised to start this project, hopefully in October 2000. It is envisaged that fundraising events will continue to be organised by the Church.

This is a very worthwhile project for all of us to celebrate the Millennium.

Weston Village TG Annual Report 1998/9

Number 13 is a lucky one for the **Bridge Group** as this is the number of ladies who regularly enjoy weekly sessions at their new venue, Fairfield House. They continued their "exchange visits" with friends from Bristol and Weston-super-Mare, a practice that has been enjoyed for twenty years and entered the Federation national heat. An innovation this year was celebration of the Chinese New Year at Fairfield House.

The **Choir** has entertained on several occasions throughout the year despite falling numbers. Residents at Stratton House, Newbridge Court and Partis College, where a magnificent collection of £75.50 was given to Guild charities, enjoyed their singing at our May meeting. They produced their usual high standard of music at our Carol Service but it has been decided that in future this is the only occasion when the whole choir will sing. Instead some members have formed a "Songsters" group, which will concentrate on music in a lighter vein. They have received an enthusiastic reception at the Salvation Army Home, the Autumn Leaves Club, Bridgemead House, the Guild Christmas party and the joint May Evening with the Drama Group.

The **Discussion Group** met to discuss the three National Council Meeting motions: the legalisation of cannabis for medicinal purposes; discrimination against women representatives to the Olympic Games by certain countries; and compulsory voting at general and local elections.

The **Drama Group** has had a difficult year with illness amongst members and their families. Despite this they continued to meet whenever possible and were pleased to stage "A May Evening" of drama, readings, music and songs with the newly-formed "Songsters" at the Parish Hall in aid of Guild charities. The group enjoyed a Christmas meal at Bathwick Boatman.

Joan Wilton took over the reins of the **Gardening Group** and organised a programme of events on the second Tuesday of each month, which included general garden discussions, videos of Madeira and Hampton Court Flower Show, Christmas flower arranging, a visit to the American Museum to see typical American Christmas decorations and a talk by Stan Hitt, former Bath Parks Director, on getting ready for spring. A Christmas lunch was enjoyed at Newbridge Boathouse.

It has been a somewhat frustrating year for the **History Group**. Members have reached a point where they now want to go to print one way or another. It has been decided that it will be either a very low-key "Guild" publication or a different publisher will be approached with a view to a wider circulation. Una McCullough is currently in contact with some members of Moravian Church who are keen to provide more information. She is hopeful that we shall publish before the year 2000!

Once again there was an excellent choice of **Outings** on offer from Suzette James and Marilyn Lewis, starting with a walk by the river led by Peter Ward.

This was followed by a day out at Malvern to see a brilliant Spring Flower Show. We also enjoyed a conducted walk around the Botanical Gardens with Stan Hitt, a mystery tour which ended up with supper in a wet and windy Weston-super-Mare for our June meeting, a very windy but hugely enjoyable trip to Avebury led by Basil Price, a trip to the Theatre Royal to see "Guys and Dolls" and finally an eventful Christmas shopping trip to Cheltenham.

Falling numbers caused the **Keep Fit Group** to re-think their finances last year. They have come up with new payment rules and an enthusiastic nucleus of members hope they can keep going.

The **Walking Group** members used the excuse of planning a programme of walks for the year to go to the Bathwick Boatman for a meal. They decided that each member and husband would select a month in which they would lead a walk. They must have had a very good meal that evening judging by their programme which took them to Blaise Castle, Pensford, Chipping Sodbury, Bradford-on-Avon, Keynsham – complete with four grandchildren, Wellow and Hinton Charterhouse, Weston and environs, Horningsham and Longleat, Radstock and Kilmersdon plus a weekend in the New Forest with the bonus of superb weather. The 1999 programme was planned during a dinner at The Inn at Freshford,

Our **Catering** ladies, the two Joans, have not only provided service with a smile throughout the year, they have also thought of ways of improving the service of drinks at monthly meetings. To this end we now have some splendid new coffeepots and a rearranged service area, which seems to be working very well. With the assistance of members they have provided refreshments at the Beetle Drive, Easter and Christmas coffee mornings, the Drama Group/Songsters' May Evening, the Christmas party and the Carol Service at Moravian Church. In addition they coordinated a comprehensive hot and cold buffet style Harvest Supper and organised the Birthday Dinner at Lansdown Golf Club.

Press Officer, Guin Slade, gets cross when Bath Chronicle prints our Guild name wrongly, but on the whole those notices that have been published have been satisfactory.

Vida Lees, as **Sunshine Fund** representative, has had a very busy year with a lot of sickness amongst members. But on a happier note she presented a card and plant to Liz Maynard, one of our founder members, to mark her 80th birthday in January.

Speakers

Yet another talented speaker from our own ranks got the new Guild year off to a good start at the AGM. Audrey Tinkler told us about her family's experiences when "Dining with Dukes" and I understand has had several requests to speak to other Guilds as a result. Rosaline Addicott, a quietly spoken farmer's wife from Corston, told us about how she was inspired to "Send a Cow to Uganda" which has grown into a national charity, and of her continued involvement in the advancement of rural women in that country. A very thought provoking talk by a remarkable lady. "The History of Newton Park College" was Felicity Medcalf's topic and she very kindly followed this up with two evenings of conducted walks around the college and grounds.

We learned the advantages of reflexology, aromatherapy and massage, the importance of wearing the right footwear in Japan, how to keep your cool when giving a talk on veterinary practice and every other slide in your projector jams, the beauty of the Tudor Rose, Wessex Water and its involvement in Water Aid in the third world and the colourful history of Blackmore and Langdons nurseries. 1998 ended with our usual Christmas party when we were entertained by our "Songsters" and a quiz compiled by Roy and Una McCullough. TG may be a women's organisation but what would we do without the men?

Charity Fund Raising

In November we were delighted to hand over cheques of £500 each to Rhona Cockle, the local representative of "Breakthrough' for research into breast cancer and Helen Storey representing 'Crossroads" a local charity providing care for carers. In addition we donated the proceeds from the sale of coffee and mince pies at the Carol Service to the Goodwill Children's Village whilst selling £100 worth of cards made locally for this same organisation. Charity fund raising remains an important part of Guild activities and we enjoy ourselves whilst so doing. Current charities are the Ultrasound Scanner Appeal for the Cancer Unit at Royal United Hospital, Bath Stroke Association and Research into Multiple Sclerosis and we are up to £800 already.

Activities

Vida Lees again represented us in the local heat of the National Scrabble competition while Captain Brenda Smith steered her team into the second round of the Federation Skittles Competition. There was better attendance at the Birthday Dinner at Lansdown Golf Club so we are returning there this year. It is close to Weston, they have a lovely room and ample parking and most people were happy with their food. Continuing on the food theme, numbers were disappointing for the Harvest Supper, despite a sumptuous buffet. However, an evening of good food and dancing all for a fiver was thoroughly enjoyed by those who did attend.

We enjoyed a Beetle Drive in February and a Walking Treasure Hunt in July organised by Una and Mary followed by supper at Una's daughter's home in Corsham – a clever ploy that foxed some participants! Four more gardens were open for inspection on a wet August afternoon followed by cream teas at Pauline Hindle's.

We were represented by Janet Taylor and Joan Loxton at the National Council Meeting in Birmingham.

Weston Flower Show would be the poorer were it not for Guild members. Every year a high proportion of winners come from our ranks, especially Primrose Sawyer who wins most of the cups and surely must be "Queen of the Show".

Contacting the Townswomen's Guild

Weston Village Townswomen's Guild meets on the third Wednesday of each month at the Moravian Church Hall at 7.30pm, and is always keen to welcome new members.

The Guild offers a variety of activities and outings and new members would be invited to join in pursuits such as drama, choir, gardening, bridge, scrabble, local history, skittles, topical discussion and walking.

More information is available from the Secretary, Brenda Smith, on 01225 423341 or on the Weston Web at http://www.westonweb.co.uk

The Weston Web

The Weston Web is the new community web site for Weston Village, and includes news and views about Weston, and an events listing. There is also a directory of shops, pubs, medical facilities, services, clubs, societies and organisations in Weston.

The site is changing and evolving all the time, and we are constantly on the look out for your input and news, whatever it may be.

Take a look at Weston Web at the library, where internet access is free to library members, or phone Weston Web on 01225 484063.

Weston Web — www.westonweb.co.uk